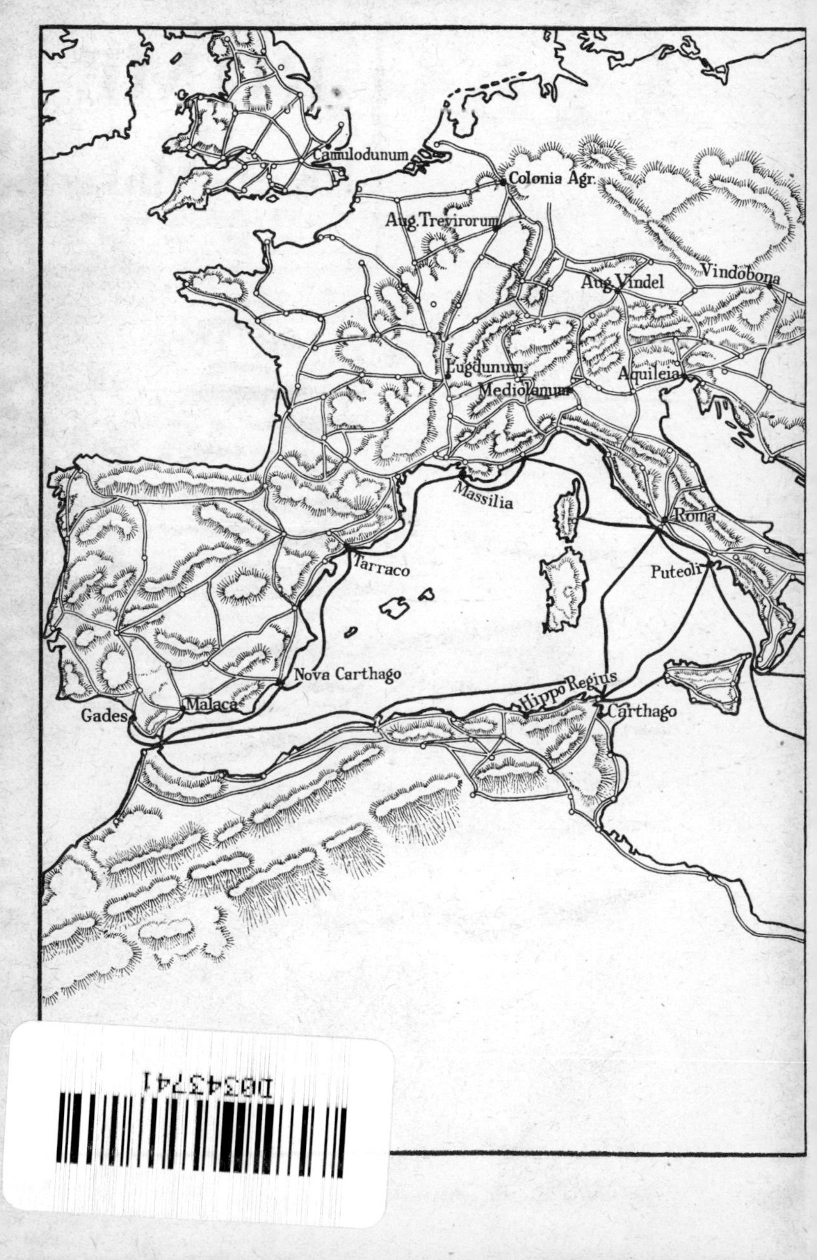
Camulodunum
Colonia Agr.
Aug. Trevirorum
Aug. Vindel
Vindobona
Lugdunum
Mediolanum
Aquileia
Massilia
Roma
Tarraco
Puteoli
Nova Carthago
Hippo Regius
Malaca
Gades
Carthago

UNIVERSITY OF NOTTINGHAM
60 0403586 5
WITHDRAWN
FROM THE LIBRARY

Superscription of the copy of Augustus's *Acts* inscribed on the temple at Ancyra.

The Growth of
ROME

BY

P. E. MATHESON

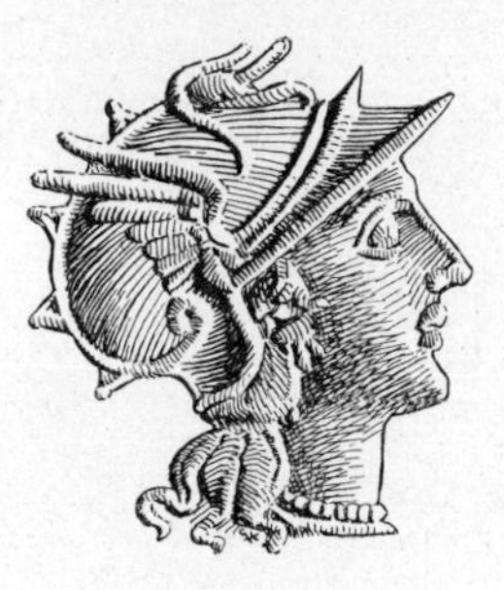

LONDON
OXFORD UNIVERSITY PRESS
HUMPHREY MILFORD
1922

PREFACE

This small volume does not pretend to be more than an attempt to suggest some of the chief characteristics that give its significance to the story of ancient Rome. It is obvious that in such a sketch much must be omitted and that it is impossible to enter in detail into controversial questions. It is assumed that the reader has already read or will read with it one of the continuous histories which are accessible to English readers; Mommsen, Heitland, Myres, How and Leigh, and J. Wells for the Republic, and Bury and Stuart Jones for the Empire.

It is a bold venture to try to bring within the compass of some eighty pages the main features of Roman history. Such an attempt involves vast omissions, and must at the best give a very imperfect impression of what ancient Rome has meant and still means in the history of the world; but it may perhaps serve to interest readers unfamiliar with the story and stimulate them to further study. If so, its purpose will have been achieved.

All that can be done within these narrow limits is to give some slight sketch of the process by which Rome acquired the mastery first over Italy and then over the Mediterranean, and of the means by which the Romans gained and secured their Empire; to trace in some measure the secret of these successes, and to indicate the causes which ultimately led to the dissolution of the great fabric of the Empire.

The first chapter deals with the early history of Rome down to 266 B.C.: the second with the period of foreign conquest, with its reaction on the politics and constitution of Rome: the third with the decline of Senatorial government and with the period of revolution, and the fourth with the foundation and history of the Principate, from Augustus to Marcus Aurelius.

Permission to reproduce the beautiful drawings by E. Lear, Francis Towne, John Robert Cozens, and Guy Head, we owe to the courtesy of the Trustees of the British Museum.

The Growth of
R O M E

I

Roman History down to 266 B.C. *The Conquest of Italy*

Rome at the outset was one of many scores of Italian communities scattered over Italy, each living its own isolated life. It became in the end the centre of a world-wide government, the symbol of peace and order for thousands of self-governing cities dispersed over the world. The history of Rome, like the story of every people, may be looked at from two points of view. It may be viewed as an outward growth, an expansive process measurable in time and space, or it may be viewed as a spiritual development, the formation of a national character, and its embodiment in literature, art, and institutions. It may be summed up on the one hand as the building up through a thousand years of a great material structure, of a complex of states under one control and governed from one centre; on the other hand as the creation of an ideal of government, of the gradual embodiment of principles of justice in the great monuments of Roman law, the Digest and the Code, and in the great literary achievements of the Latin world, finding their culmination in the *Aeneid* of Virgil, whose spirit passed on into Latin Christianity, to inspire Augustine's City of God and Dante's vision of the Mediaeval Empire. We are accustomed to look to Greece and the Greek people as the source of creative ideas in art, science, and speculation, but we have always to remember that it was through the Roman rule and through

Roman institutions that the genius of Greece was enabled ultimately to exert its influence over a wider field and to become a formative element in the whole of western civilization. For the world which Rome ruled when her power was once established in the Mediterranean was a Graeco-Roman world. The peace which the Principate of Augustus gave to the distracted countries of Europe and the nearer East was a peace which embraced peoples speaking many languages and dialects, but among them Greek held a place by the side of Latin, and both alike were the speech of all educated men. Therefore we cannot think of Greek and Roman history apart, and we shall see that, long before the *Pax Augusti*, the reaction of Greece on Rome had begun to mould political movements and to determine the direction of literary evolution. It is significant that two of the books which have done most for our familiar knowledge of the Roman world are written in Greek—Plutarch's *Lives* and the New Testament. But this does not mean that Rome has not its distinctive character and development. It is this development which I now propose to try to trace.

Our knowledge of the earlier history of Rome is unfortunately based on very inadequate evidence. It is not until the second century B.C. that we have in Polybius, the Greek statesman and exile, a historian writing on contemporary events: further back we are dependent on secondhand historians, such as Livy, and on what we can derive from such documents as the list of consuls, the remains of the legal document known as the XII Tables, and such inferences as may be drawn from the evidence of language, from later institutions, civil and religious, and from the discoveries of the archaeologist in Rome and Italy. But the main outlines of the early history are fairly clear.

As a preliminary, one glance at the geography is necessary.

Politically Italy was not a united whole until the close of the Republic, but throughout the history which culminated in that union, its geographical unity and its local diversities had an important influence on the political development. Beneath the great barrier of the Alps in the north is the rich plain of Lombardy; open to attack from east and west—over the low passes of the Maritime Alps on the west and of Istria on the east. From this fertile alluvial plain the great chain of the Apennines stretches along the full length of the peninsula. Only in Etruria, Umbria, Latium, and Campania is there any extensive plain country; and in the extreme south-west in Bruttium the peninsula ends in the wildest forest. The enormous length of the peninsula, in Roman days as now, made communications and a unified administration very difficult. But Rome had from the outset the supreme advantage of central position in the peninsula and a commanding site on the Tiber. From this central position she could gradually extend her power north and south, over the plains of Etruria and Latium, and later to the wider plains beyond. Throughout the story we have to remember the permanent geographical conditions and also the variety of Italian life—the contrast of plain and mountain, which provide the winter and summer pastures; the contrast between town and country life, between the austerer Sabine highlands and the rich plains of Lombardy or Latium and Campania. The aspect of the land has been altered since Roman times by the cutting down of forests and the silting up of rivers—the ancient crops of spelt have given place first to wheat and later to olive and vine, and later again to maize—but hundreds of towns remain on the same sites as in Roman days, and the Italian cattle to-day move to and fro along the same immemorial green tracks from plain to mountain and from mountain to plain.

At the beginning of the historic period we have to imagine the peninsula occupied by a large number of separate communities, some with a civic, some with a tribal organization: Greek cities in the extreme south; a Celtic or, as the Romans called them, a Gallic population in the north, pressing down on the Etruscan peoples who had occupied a good part of Lombardy and Venetia and who were still in undisputed possession of Tuscany. There were also the Ligurian tribes along the Western Riviera, and, occupying the central region, were the two main branches of the distinctively Italian races, the Latins and the Umbro-Sabellians; the Latins with their centre in the region south of the Tiber, the Umbro-Sabellians, including in the north the Umbrians, and farther south the Sabines, Samnites, and Lucanians, spreading down from the Celtic country to the Greek region of the south and already threatening the existence of the Greek cities. These Greek cities, it must always be remembered, had maintained their own distinctive Greek life in contact with the cities of Sicily and the mainland of Greece, whose trade and civilization they shared.

The compact solidarity of the united Italy which ultimately came into being under the governing guidance of Rome is partly due to the fact that the Celts, the Greeks, and the Italian peoples were not alien from one another in race, and that in particular the Celts and the Italians were closely related, and well fitted to complement each other's qualities and form by fusion a strong and resourceful people. But the process was a gradual one. The unity of Italy was only consummated at the accession of Augustus, and when it became merged as time went on in the great machine of the Empire, its national unity was lost, not to appear again till the Risorgimento.[1] What

[1] See Dr. J. W. Mackail, *The Italy of Virgil and the Italy of Dante*, in Dante, Essays in Commemoration, London University Press, 1921.

we have to notice in this early period is that the alien elements, Etruscan and Ligurian, were absorbed without greatly affecting the Roman character, and the intercourse with the cities of the so-called ' Great Greece ' of the south prepared the way for the later stage in Roman history, when Rome became the mistress of the Graeco-Roman world. But the fusion of races was only a co-operating cause. The greatness of Rome was based ultimately on the distinctive character of her people, on qualities of manliness, discipline, and order, which marked out the inhabitants of the city on the Tiber from her Latin and Sabine kinsmen, as a conquering and governing race.

It was in the period with which we are now concerned that these qualities were developed, by quiet growth and strenuous conflict, in which the issue long seemed uncertain and only a rare union of tenacity, compromise, and political genius finally established Roman power. At the end of the period we find Rome entering the circle of the great powers by her treaty with Egypt in 273, which brought her into the main stream of Mediterranean history. We have now to trace the process by which this great position was achieved.

In the earliest period we have to think of the Roman State as a small community established on the hills [1] above the Tiber, with the Palatine as its centre : a community consisting, according to the tradition, of a mingling of Latin and Sabine elements. The people are mainly agricultural, but from very early days they maintained maritime and commercial relations with the outside world through the settlement of Ostia at the river's mouth. The period before 266 B.C. falls into two main divisions. The Roman Republic, like that of Athens, was preceded by a period of monarchy which is said to have lasted

[1] The annual festival of the *Septimontium* on December 11 marks the significance of the hills in the early history.

some two hundred and forty years, down to 509 B.C. In that period, among the uncertain shadows of legendary history we can already trace certain significant features. First there was the expiring effort of the Etruscan power in Italy expressed in a period of Etruscan rule or influence in Rome. That influence disappeared and left no trace except in some of the religious institutions of the city and in the world of art. Secondly, we see the beginnings of a constitutional government in which an assembly of the people already played an important part. Thirdly, Rome had already begun to acquire a dominant position in the League of the Latin Cities. And finally, the firm foundations were already beginning to be laid of Roman law and legal procedure.

Certain names were handed down from this period, which were associated with the origin of the religious and civil institutions of Rome, and in particular that of King Servius Tullius, to whom are attributed two momentous changes: (1) the new organization of the people for military purposes, the origin of the great assembly of citizens, the *Comitia Centuriata*; (2) the alliance with the Latins, the outward symbol of which was the temple of Diana on the Aventine. The walls, which are attributed to him, are probably not earlier than the fourth century B.C. This great formative period, with no literature and very uncertain records, was no doubt of immense importance in giving shape to Roman character and direction to Roman institutions, but it remains shadowy and obscure.

With the fall of the Monarchy in 509 and the foundation of the Republic we pass into a clearer air, although for some century and a half the records are still far from certain. The two hundred and forty years from 509 to 266, saw the foundations laid of the civil and military system of the Republic. It saw also the expansion of Roman power over the central regions of the Italian peninsula, until at the close Rome had mastered her neighbours to north and south, and had created the nucleus of a great Italian union of states, owning her supremacy, and privileged to share, as time went on, her expanding trade and her governing position.

Let us look first at the internal development.

The factors in the constitution which followed on the period of the kings define themselves clearly from the first and determine the future of Rome.[1]

The executive is in the hands of two annual magistrates, possessing full power, *imperium*, both civil and military, each magistrate having power to veto the other's acts. It is on this executive power that ultimately the government of Italy and the Empire depends. Whether they are called Praetors, as at first, or Consuls, the name we are familiar with in history, this pair of magistrates represents the characteristic executive of Rome. It is only on special occasions, for military or formal purposes, that recourse is had to the nomination of a Dictator by one of the Consuls. The Dictator is an emergency officer who acts for a limited time, and is never regarded as a normal official of the State. It is in the two annual Consuls, commanding the armies and administering the affairs of the city, that the effective force of the State resides. Their Imperium, or civil and military command, is the organic cell, so to say, from which all the governing greatness of Rome was evolved. The Magistrates are the creation of the people, the Populus Romanus, the whole assembled body of citizens.

In this Populus Romanus we find already distinctions which are significant through history. We see, first, the distinction

[1] For constitutional questions see A. J. Greenidge, *Roman Public Life*, which embodies the substance of Mommsen's *Staatsrecht*, independently handled.

of master and dependant, or patron and client ; and, secondly, the distinction, vastly more important for political purposes, of Patrician and Plebeian. The Patricians were the members of the select families, who alone could be fathers of their family in the full sense and alone could share in the older worships of the State. The Plebeians, or Plebs, were those outside this inner circle, originally unprivileged and many of them poor. These outsiders gradually, as time went on, acquired a special assembly of their own and absolute social and political equality with the Patricians, except that to the end they were shut out from some of the sacred offices, in particular that of *Rex sacrorum*, which belong to the original inner families of the community. The Populus Romanus is the ultimate sovereign, the ultimate source of power, for legislation and for election of magistrates, and for the exercise of the final deciding vote in criminal cases. Whether they met by *Curiae*, or wards, as in the early days of the city or by *Centuries*, the military ordering of the people which is attributed to the legendary king Servius Tullius, but may belong to a later date, or by *Tribes*, the district divisions which in the later Republic are the important civic unit, they vote always not as individuals but in groups, and their effective voting power depends very much on the arrangement of the groups. But besides Consuls and People there is that august assembly, which becomes, as time goes on, the seat and centre of Roman government, i.e. the Senate. Fundamental to the Roman mind is the duty of the magistrate to take advice from the wise. The Senate is the Council which it is the duty of the Consuls to consult, and in proportion as the power of Rome extends and the Citizen Assembly less and less corresponds to the whole body of Roman citizens, the power of the Senate grows, till it becomes the commanding factor in the constitution.

Before this point was reached, new magistracies had grown up around the original pair. There were the Censors (443), periodical officers at five years' interval to take the census, choose men into the Senate, and exercise a general supervision over manners. More important because they were elected yearly were the Praetors,[1] who administered justice. Through them and through their edicts was built up the law of Rome, and by an extension of their office the office of provincial governor was developed. The Praetors, too, can also act as heads of the Government if the Consuls are away. Various minor magistrates too appear—Quaestors, the officials for finance, and Aediles, concerned with the internal economics of Rome. Thus, by a process of division and differentiation, the original executive of the single king is broken up into groups of specialized officials; the monarchy is put in commission.

Outside these offices there was another group which must be mentioned apart: the Plebeians by degrees had become an organized power in the State, their officers, the Tribunes of the Plebs, originally merely the officers of a corporation within the State, became practically magistrates of Rome, but with distinctive attributes which mark their position as different from that of the Magistrates proper. Their powers are not Command (Imperium) but Auxilium (Help) on the one hand, and on the other, the negative power of intercession or veto, which enabled them to block and so to control legislation. In the first two centuries of the Republic these officers, who are elected by the Plebeian Assembly (*Concilium Plebis*

[1] The Praetors, like our English Judges, did not decide questions of fact. They laid down the law and referred the question of fact to a *iudex* or *iudices*. They did not even direct the jury, but by consulting wise men of the law they brought theory to bear on practice.

Tributum), have the power of summoning and presiding over this Assembly, and acquire for it by degrees the full legislative power. The Hortensian Law of 287 put them finally for law-making purposes on the level of the Populus Romanus, while a Licinian law of 367, eighty years earlier, had already secured for the Plebs one place at least in the consulate each year. The effect of this was momentous.

The Plebs, the Commons, thus enfranchized are not to be regarded as merely a poor and dependent class : from almost the earliest days they consisted of richer and poorer elements. The process which culminated in the Licinian and the Hortensian laws may be regarded from two points of view. On the one hand it was a widening of the conception of citizenship. The Citizen body now came to include all elements of the people, voting in their Tribes in equality side by side. On the other hand the process was an enlargement of the circle of the nobility from whose ranks the magistrates were drawn, and of the Senate into which they passed after holding office. Thus the earlier nobility of birth passed in the fourth century into a nobility of office, consisting of those families whose ancestors had held the higher magistracies.

To a date early in the Republican period, 450 B. C., is referred the institution of the Twelve Tables, which were looked back to as the foundation of Roman Law.[1] Though the circumstances which surround them are mixed with legendary elements there can be no doubt that the establishment of a written code marks a definite stage in the development of Rome ; it is clear from the evidence we have of them that they represent the principles and practice of a primitive age.

This is the history of the State from within. Let us now look without. These earlier centuries record a series of

[1] 'Fons omnis publici privatique est iuris', *Liv.* iii. 34.

View from above Ponte Nomentano near the Mons Sacer, by Francis Towne.

conflicts with the races of Italy in which Rome met, and after repeated failures overcame, the armed forces of her neighbours, Etruscans and Gauls in the north, the mountain races in the near east and south—Sabines and Volscians and Hernicans—the Samnites and the Greek cities in the south.

These conflicts are recorded for us by late historians, in whose pages wars and battles are often duplicated, but certain facts emerge clearly from the legendary darkness. First is the fact that Rome's central position was at the outset established by her control and domination of the great League of the Latin cities. The stages of her progress are marked by certain critical moments. These were the destruction of Alba Longa in the period of the monarchy, the closing of the League against new members in 385, and the dissolution of the League in 338. Rome's relations with these Latin communities left their mark far on into the Empire. By the destruction of Alba Longa, the old capital of the League of the Latin towns, Rome had become the dominant power in it. Then by exercising her control over the members of the League, Rome founded under its auspices new centres of influence in the colonies of the League. It was these early colonies which formed a model for the later 'Latin colonies' which, when Rome had become supreme, she herself founded as garrisons to control the great roads that led north and south and held the peninsula in their inevitable grip. And later on when these colonies in Italy had become merged in the Roman State, the Latin status, *Latinitas* or *Latium*, was still bestowed on towns beyond the seas as a preliminary stage towards the grant of full Roman citizenship. Such towns formed centres of Roman influence in the provinces.

The League also left a striking religious survival in the Roman State in the form of the great Latin Festival, which was celebrated every year by the Consuls at the opening of

The Lake of Nemi near Alba Longa, by John Robert Cozens.

their year of office in the temple of Juppiter Latiaris, Jove of the Latins, on the top of the Alban Mount.[1] It is a thrilling spot even now. Before Rome's control over the Latin towns was established the city of Rome had to suffer the ignominy of a Gallic raid, which gave the Celts of the north possession of the city for a short time, and left to tradition the legend of the geese of the Capitol. It is only after the recovery of the city and the re-establishment of order that the records of Roman history begin to be established on a solid basis. The domination over Latium was only the beginning of Rome's struggle for mastery. The records of the earlier years of the Republic are full of repeated conflicts with the Etruscan cities across the Tiber on the north, particularly the city of Veii. This city, about twelve miles north of Rome, threatened for generations the very existence of the city on the Tiber, and its conquest in 396 by the heroic M. Furius Camillus, the first great name in the external history of Rome, marks a decisive moment in Rome's advance. The sequel to his victory was the foundation of two Latin colonies at Sutrium and Nepĕte, *the gates of Etruria*, in 383.

The conflicts with the hill-tribes of the south and east, the Aequians and the Volscians, were no less significant. These tribes inhabited the hilly country east and south of that group of volcanic hills, the Alban Mountains, with which visitors to Rome are familiar as closing the southern view from Rome.

The traveller who goes south-eastwards to Velletri (Velitrae), twenty-five miles from Rome, and from there climbs Mount Algidus, the southern outpost of the Alban hills, can see about him the sites of the hill-towns of Tusculum to the north and

[1] This historic temple on the top of Monte Cavo made way for a monastery in the eighteenth century.

Praeneste (now Palestrina) to the south-east, and below him can mark the point where the Latin road runs through the pass of the Alban hills into the heart of the Volscian country. From this outpost it may be seen how the support of the Latins and of the Hernicans enabled Rome to fight and subdue the Volscians. We have a glimpse of the struggle in the legend of Coriolanus, familiar to all from Shakespeare's play. The victory was won partly by arms and partly by diplomacy.

It was only when this hill country had been conquered that Rome was able to become independent of her allies. The last Latin war ended, as we have seen, in the dissolution of the Latin League in 338. This marks the final collapse of Latin resistance. Rome to all intents and purposes had swallowed up Latium. This closed the first great stage in the process by which Rome became supreme head of an Italian Confederation, which in the end was conterminous with the Italian peninsula. It was only then, with Southern Etruria subdued beyond the Tiber and Latium as a solid base to work from, that the further advance southwards became possible.

Eighty years earlier, in 420, the Campanian Samnites, Sabine tribes attracted by the wealth and civilization of the Greek cities of the south, had pushed down the peninsula and conquered Cumae—the oldest Greek settlement in Italy. The fall of Cumae struck a warning note for the other Greek cities. More recently, in 341, Rome had made alliance with the Samnites, but now that Rome had completed her mastery over the Latin towns a conflict with Samnium was inevitable, unless Rome was to accept the control of Magna Graecia by the Sabellian races. The victory of the Samnites would have meant a divided Italy, half Latin and half Oscan, unable to hold its own against Carthage or other great powers. For between fifty and sixty years (347–290) Rome was engaged, with intervals of peace, in a great struggle with this powerful race. It was a war of the city of the plain matched against the people of the mountains, with their own language and civilization and their own ambitions. The first stage ended with the foundation of the great fortress of Luceria (a Latin colony of 2,500 colonists, founded in 314), followed by similar fortresses in Apulia and Campania and the construction of the great south road, the Via Appia, in 312. In the next twenty years the Samnites found support at different times in the Etruscans, the Hernicans, and other races of central Italy, whose resistance made necessary the further consolidation of Rome's position by roads and colonies. The most critical moment was the great battle of Sentinum, 295, in Umbria, on the borders of the Celtic country, east of the Flaminian road. On that famous battle-field the Umbrians, Etruscans, and Gauls of the north fought side by side with the Samnites against Rome, and were defeated. This battle decisively broke the alliance between Rome's northern and southern enemies. The great roads and colonies established a solid block of Romanized land between the Celtic and the Samnite countries. Even after this great victory the position of Rome was not yet completely secure. The Sabine country indeed was absorbed into the Roman citizenship, but Etruscans and Gauls took up war again and Rome had still to reckon with the Greek cities of the south which she had for a time defended against the attacks of the Lucanians, also a Samnite people. The collision came in 282. Tarentum, that town whose deep and spacious harbour is now familiar to our soldiers and sailors as Taranto, had become the dominant State in the south, and secured the help of Pyrrhus, king of Epirus beyond the Adriatic, to defend her against attack. For a time it looked as if this brilliant adventurer, by his victories in Italy and Sicily, might carve out a new Greek power in the south. But Pyrrhus was too far from his base across the Adriatic; his nearer allies, too, the Greek cities of Sicily failed to support him, for united action among Greek cities was always hard to secure. The war ended in the submission of Tarentum on honourable terms and the collapse of the Samnite resistance in the south. Twice again Rome had to meet the resistance of the Samnites. They gave support to Hannibal after his great victory at Cannae, and in the civil wars of Marius and Sulla they again fought against Rome, only to be butchered after the battle of the Colline Gate.

Thus by a series of wars Rome had become head of a great confederation of various but mainly kindred races, but it is in the means by which her rule was established and confirmed that her genius is best seen.

The first principle of Roman rule was: *Divide et impera*—divide to conquer. Rome tolerated no league or alliance between tribes or cities. With each of her allies and subjects she made a separate treaty: no city or tribe could have its own foreign policy, none could combine with any other. They were all separate units. They had different grades of privilege and were kept apart by their difference. Rome alone could make war or treaties, and although coins might be struck at other mints besides that of Rome they bore Roman emblems and were of Roman standard.[1] It is significant that in 269 the silver *denarius*, of which we still retain a record in the symbol *d* for our penny, was introduced as the unit of Rome's imperial currency, to remain so for over five hundred years.[2] If we look beyond Rome and those towns of Latium which had the full franchise, we find a group of towns which had Roman citizenship, but without the power

[1] G. F. Hill, *Historical Roman Coins*, p. 17. [2] Ibid., p. 28.

of voting in the Assembly (*civitas sine suffragio*). Their citizens served in the legions and shared the burdens and private rights of Roman citizenship.[1] Some of these towns governed themselves, others had justice administered to them by a prefect from Rome. This was a transitional type of citizenship, which had disappeared in five or six generations, before the final struggle for the franchise—the Social War of 91–89. Beyond these semi-privileged communities come the mass of the Allied States (*civitates foederatae*), who governed themselves and sent their own contingents in squadrons of horse and cohorts of foot to fight side by side with the Roman legionaries. They paid no money tribute to Rome. The cities with Latin rights, the 'Latin name' as they were called, were a special class of those Allies, who shared in the private rights of citizens, and could if they chanced to be in Rome when the Citizen Assemblies met, give a vote in that Assembly.[2] They could also by migrating to Rome or by serving a magistracy in their own town acquire the full franchise of Rome.

The important thing to notice is that in her dealings with the Italians Rome combined strong and effective control with the lavish grant of valuable and varied privileges to her allies, and thus made easy and natural the process of gradual incorporation and fusion. It is this inclusive and far-seeing policy, at once liberal and strong, which marks her political superiority to Athens, where the confederacy of allies degenerated into an Empire, and to Sparta, which always kept the Lacedaemonian population in subjection.[3]

[1] The technical name for this status was *municipium*, see Greenidge, *Roman Public Life*, p. 304. After the social war *municipium* is the general term for a self-governing community possessing Roman or Latin rights.

[2] Cf. *Liv.* xxv. 3.

[3] Mr. Strachan Davidson used to quote Mr. W. L. Newman as saying that 'Sparta never ennobled the Perioecic relation'.

Throughout this period of conquest there was going on a process of Romanization by means of colonies and roads of which the chief were the great southern road (*Via Appia*) and the great northern road (*Via Flaminia*), secured by fortresses which were Latin colonies possessing the rights already described. The colonists sent there, varying in number from 2,000 to 20,000 (Venusia), consisted of conquered Italians or of Roman settlers, who were ready to give up their full citizen rights and accept the Latin status in return for allotments on the conquered land.[1] Even in this early period some colonies were founded with full Roman citizenship, but it was only later in the second century B.C., when the position of the Italians had deteriorated, that the Latin colonies give way to the Roman.[2] This double process, extension of citizenship and extension of Latin rights, is to be traced in the record of (1) new tribes, until the final number of thirty-five was reached in the year 241; and (2) new Latin colonies, mainly on the great roads, in Etruria and Umbria, the Volscian country, and the highlands of the Marsians and the Aequians.

The foundation and background of Italian life was still agricultural: farming was the main industry, both citizens and non-citizens looked to this for their living. The organization of the army as we trace it in the divisions of the Centuriate Assembly shows that there is inequality of property at an early date, and we have to imagine large estates, side by side with small farms; but it was not till the prolonged wars of foreign conquest took the yeomen farmers away from their farms for many months together that the evil of *latifundia*, that is, large

[1] Travellers on the railway between Piacenza (Placentia) and Modena (Mutina) may still trace the parallel lines of the allotments as laid out by the Roman commissioners and surveyors.

[2] Aquileia, 181 B.C., was the last Latin colony in Italy.

estates run by slave labour, and crushing out the smaller farmers, began to be a crying grievance. In this earlier period the main life of the people is a country life. The commerce of the seas had in the dawn of Roman history been still in the hands of the Etruscans on the west and of the Greek cities Corinth and Athens and Corcyra on the east; but in the western seas Carthage, which for generations had been exercising pressure on the Greek cities of Sicily and Southern Italy, was now taking the place of the Etruscans. The Etruscan cities had received a fatal blow from Syracuse in 474, and by the middle of the fourth century (and possibly 150 years earlier) Rome was making a treaty with Carthage (348). By that treaty the Romans agreed to recognize the western sphere of influence of Carthage in Spain and Africa in return for receiving the privileges of free trade in Sicily and protection for the Italian coast towns from Punic attack. The position of Italy with its long sea-board on both sides, then, as to-day, made her relations with countries possessing sea-power of vast importance, and it was becoming clear that sooner or later Rome would have to obtain the command of both the upper and the lower waters—the Adriatic and the Tuscan Sea. But so far Rome was too much occupied in the absorption and consolidation of her conquests in Central Italy to do more than temporize with the maritime states of the day. Her treaty with Carthage in 306, which limited Roman activity in the southern seas, was dictated by the pressure of the Samnite wars, and it was not till the conquest of Southern Italy was complete that the Romans could enter on the conflict for sea power with the great commercial city state of Africa.

If we look back on these early centuries and ask the secret of Roman success we find it in a combination of causes—the central position of Rome, the fighting quality of her people which was able to maintain an efficient fighting force of two to four legions, or more when occasion called, composed of soldiers who were not mercenaries, like those of Carthage, nor town riff-raff, like those raised in Rome at a later date. They were strong men bred in the fields, who could ply the plough as well as the sword, and who returned from their campaigns to work on their ancient farms or on the new allotments assigned them by the government commissioners on the public land along the great high roads as a reward for service done. But these causes alone would not have sufficed: it was the political genius of Rome which made the Romans succeed in Italy as neither Etruscans nor Celts nor Greeks had done before them. If we look first to institutions we have to remember that from the earliest days of the Republic there existed in germ two institutions which were to determine the future of Rome.

The first of them, the Imperium, the high command of the consuls, was the germ out of which the elaborate system of the Roman magistracy was developed. From this was evolved, as time went on, the Praetorship with its system of Roman law, the Provincial Governorship, with its combination of civil and military command, and finally the Principate, in which the high command in the end overshadows and controls the advisory body which had in earlier days kept it in control.

Secondly, there was the Senate, the body which throughout the Republic was the most permanent element in the State. The Senate, while magistrates clash and pass away, remains to supply the continuous vital tissue of government. On this, in the last resort, and on the character, the *moral* of its members, the existence of the Republic depends. Against the power of the Senate the individual magistrate, be he Consul or Praetor or Tribune, cannot in the end prevail.

These two factors, the power of the Magistrate, the permanence and vitality of the Senate, govern the whole history. It is only in the age of revolution, when the adjustment between the two falls out of gear, when the commander has lost the habit of obedience, and when the Senate has lost its power of giving sound counsel, that the collapse of the Republic begins. But in the earlier stages, while the growth of Rome was still confined to Italy, these constitutional resources served her in good stead.

Institutions, however, are not enough without a genius for political life. Rome had a genius for politics, which showed itself in this period of political expansion in three characteristic ways.

(1) There was a sense of discipline and government, which from early times developed a sound system of law and justice and proved adaptable to the conditions of the expanding State. With this went a high average capacity for command. The wealthier families produced from year to year a succession of magistrates who, without distinguished genius, maintained a high level of public service and created from their stored experience a senatorial order in which the merits of heredity and of selection were remarkably combined.

(2) Secondly in this period of Rome's expansion we have to notice the peculiar gift which the governing class of Rome showed for handling political difficulties. From early days, as we have seen, there were conflicts between the two orders, Patrician and Plebeian, rivalries between the different Assemblies, competition for privilege and power. More than once there were secessions of the Commons which seemed to threaten the very existence of the State. But through all this period of the struggle between the orders and this violent clash of forces there prevailed a spirit of reasonable compromise which

was the making of Rome's greatness. This perhaps more than anything else is what distinguishes the political history of Rome from that of the States of Greece and gives it the stability and strength which were the foundation of its success.

(3) And thirdly the liberal policy of incorporation, the generous bestowal of the franchise, and the influence of Roman law and order, diffused by the action of the magistrates and of those who represented Rome in her relations with the Allies, were building up a moral and political fabric which was to hold together the races and classes of the Italian peninsula in a way that no power east or west of it had yet exercised in Europe.

2

The Period of Foreign Conquest (266–146) *and its Reaction on the Roman Constitution*

We have seen that Rome by a combination of military vigour and political capacity had established her position in Italy, and that no power in the peninsula was able to dispute her supremacy. That supremacy, we saw, was secured by the building of great roads and the foundation of fortress colonies which made a strong barrier between the enemies in the north and those in the south. The secret of Rome's success so far lay chiefly in the military efficiency of her soldiers and in the concentrated and compact fabric of the Senatorial order. It remained to be seen whether the same qualities would enable the Romans to rise to the height of the new task which they now began to take in hand. The problem which confronted them was that which has so profoundly moved the Italians of to-day—the problem of supremacy in the waters of the peninsula. Etruscans, Greeks, Carthaginians had hitherto competed for commerce and control in these waters and in the outlying islands of Sicily and Sardinia. The power of the Etruscans had been declining ever since their defeat by Hiero of Syracuse in 474, and long before their final submission to Rome in 280 they had been removed from the field of possible rivals. Of the Greek powers in the west Tarentum had been defeated: Syracuse, the leading state in Sicily, had from time to time put up a strong defence against the Punic settlements in that island, but never with a success complete enough either to expel these persistent Semitic settlers and traders or to establish a supremacy over South Italy. For the moment the Romans had made an alliance with Carthage (278), but only under stress of their war with Pyrrhus the king of Epirus. With the defeat and retirement of Pyrrhus in 275 and the subjection of the stubborn Samnites and Lucanians in the south, it became clear that sooner or later Rome would have to match her strength against that of Carthage, unless the Romans were to be content with having an alien sea-power continually threatening their seaboard and their commerce.

The first collision arose out of an incident at the town of Messana, on the straits that bear its name, near the famous rock of Scylla and whirlpool Charybdis, which might almost be said to typify the two influences which were struggling for supremacy in the island. By which overmastering force were these old Greek settlements to be swept away? Were they to be swallowed up by the rising power of Rome or to surrender their island at last to the menacing advance of Punic enterprise and commerce? Some Campanian soldiers of fortune, the Mamertines, who had ventured to Sicily in the reign of Agathocles (that gallant but cruel adventurer who made a near approach to achieving the expulsion of the Carthaginians from Sicily) had occupied Messana in order to form there an independent

State. They came into conflict in Messana with Hiero, king of Syracuse, and when pressed by him they appealed for help both to Rome and to Carthage. Both powers in turn intervened. Carthage at first acted alone, and then supported Hiero against the Mamertines. Rome, in spite of the help that Hiero had recently given her in Magna Graecia (271), decided to support the Mamertines and by so doing declared for the policy of supremacy in Sicily. The conflict between Carthaginians and Romans for the possession of Messana was the beginning of that first war with Carthage which for over twenty years (264–241) made large demands on the Roman resources and several times threatened completely to overwhelm the Roman State. The Romans secured the alliance of Syracuse in 263, and though some other towns of the Sicilian coast had Punic sympathies and though for some time a vigorous Punic aggressive was carried on in the west of the island under Hamilcar Barca, nevertheless the Roman forces in the end prevailed. But the cost was heavy. The Romans did indeed win several victories at sea, at Mylae in North Sicily (260), Ecnomus in South Sicily (256), and the Hermaean Cape in Africa (255), but these were balanced by great disasters from foul weather and unskilled command. The only attempt made by Rome to carry the aggressive into Africa ended in the defeat and capture of Regulus, the Roman commander, whose voluntary return to Carthage as a prisoner became a legend illustrating the heroic honour of a true Roman.[1] Without entering into the details of this war we may mention two principal features which are characteristic and deserve notice: first the dauntless tenacity of the Romans, who built fleet after fleet to repair their losses; and secondly the Roman want of seamanship as compared with the Carthaginians. The Romans had, indeed, the South Italians to draw on for their

[1] Horace, *Odes*, iii. 5.

oarsmen and sailors (and they were Greeks who had been mariners for many generations), but the Roman naval commanders were the ordinary consuls of the year. These were, of course, noblemen of average capacity and without technical skill upon the sea, and their naval tactics were in general confined to the very simple plan of converting a sea-fight into a land-fight by the help of boarding-bridges and grappling-irons. Finally, the Romans were greatly handicapped by *the system of annual command*, which made a continuous strategy impossible, while the constant shipbuilding was an immense drain on the resources of the Roman State. Finance at Rome, it must be remembered, was still elementary. The military system rested on personal service by ordinary citizens, while the armies and fleets of Carthage were purely professional. It is a striking evidence of the rudimentary state of Roman finance that the fleet which ended the war by the great victory at the Aegates Islands (241) off the western coast of Sicily was a fleet of light ships raised by voluntary contributions.

The peace forced upon Carthage by this defeat had momentous consequences not only for Rome and Carthage but for the whole Mediterranean world and for the history of Europe. It finally expelled the Semitic power from Sicily and prepared the way for the complete Romanization of the western seas. It crippled the power of Carthage by the indemnity imposed upon her, and so led almost immediately to a mutiny of the Punic mercenary troops which kept Carthage occupied at home and enabled Rome within the next five years to add Sardinia and Corsica to her domain. The western sea thus became completely Roman. Most momentous of all, it gave the Romans the final mastery over Sicily and was the beginning of a new form of government which contained the seeds of ruin for the Republic of Rome.

Sicily was the first Roman province. What does this mean? Hitherto Roman conquest had been confined to the Italian peninsula. Every conquest had been followed by a process of incorporation into the Roman State system, by which the conquered peoples acquired a share in the Roman confederacy of Italian States, subject indeed to Rome, but nominally independent and free and enjoying a certain measure of self-government. Their status gave them a place by the side of the Romans in battle and in commerce and opened up the possibility of further promotion, which enabled them as time went on to share completely or incompletely in the citizenship of Rome. The Italian allies of Rome, as we have seen, paid no tribute—their contribution to the Roman Government was in the form of personal service in the army or on shipboard.

Now mark the change which comes over the Roman State. The cities of Sicily which were now made subject to Rome, instead of being governed as part of the Italian Confederacy, whose soldiers mustered in their squadrons and cohorts to fight side by side with Roman citizens, were subject to Rome in a new sense. A Roman officer, with civil and military powers, took the place of the Carthaginian governor and later, when Syracuse was annexed, the place of the Syracusan king (201). From 227 onwards two Praetors were elected year by year at Rome to go and govern Sicily and Sardinia (with Corsica), each island being termed a province. That word is simply the name for a department or sphere of command. The Praetor, who in Rome and Italy was one among a group of colleagues who had equal powers with him and might modify his action, was in this more distant field much more like the monarch or absolute governor whom he succeeded. Again the cities of Sicily contributed money and corn to Rome instead of military service. They paid a yearly tribute. This tributary relation was significant and momentous and that in two ways: in the government of Syracuse which the Romans took over in 212, and still more in the kingdom of Pergamum which was bequeathed to Rome in 133 and which became the Roman province of Asia, the Romans came into contact with an organized bureaucratic system of Greek officials. This fact tended to react in an unhealthy way on Republican institutions at home. And the idea of a tributary State or complex of States in which there was little personal contact between governor and governed easily led to a conception of the overseas conquests of Rome as 'estates of the Roman people' to be exploited at all costs for the benefit of the governing race. The combination of this conception with the Roman system of annual appointment led to calamitous results. The transitory governor and his finance officer, the Quaestor, were but birds of passage and could have no real intimacy with their transitory subjects.

There was, indeed, some graduation of rights and privileges among the inhabitants. The Sicilian province, like the later provinces of Rome, was not a uniform dead-level surface. Of the sixty-eight communities which Rome governed there eight were treated either as allied or as free and untaxed. Of the remainder some continued to pay the tithe of their produce (wine, oil, and corn) which they had paid to their previous ruler; some were deprived of their land, which became domain-land of the Roman people, '*ager publicus populi Romani*', and cultivated it as tenants of Rome. These also appear to have paid the rent of their arable land in the form of tithe. The other taxes payable to Rome were a tax on pasture (*scriptura*) and also harbour-dues (*portorium*). The collection of these two taxes was leased by the Censors at Rome to public contractors (*publicani*), whose companies found a lucrative field in such undertakings. It was the privilege of the tithe-paying subjects in Sicily that the tithes were leased district by district in Sicily itself, and were thus managed locally. In the province of Asia, annexed eighty years later, the tithes were leased to contractors in Rome with disastrous results. The contractors paid a lump sum for the tax and then made what they could of it. In theory, it is true, the subjects were protected by the charter of the province, the *lex provinciae* drawn up by Roman commissioners at the time of annexation, but there was a wide door open to corruption, if the governor was wanting in firmness and a sense of justice. What the practical results of such a system were we see very clearly from the speeches and letters of Cicero in the first century B.C. His friendship with the capitalist contractors, the Equites, did not blind him altogether to the abuses which their uncontrolled power entailed, although it led him on occasion to sacrifice justice to friendship.

On the other side of the account it must be remembered that from the outset the conquerors provided for the administration of justice by the establishment of circuits of assize. Roman justice, though it might sometimes fail or be perverted by bribery, was, if honestly administered, a real boon to the subject peoples. In many countries it was an advance on their previous condition.

These arrangements for Sicily were not completed until thirty years later, in the middle of the second war with Carthage; but they were the direct result of the battle of the Aegates Islands and mark in a sense [1] a critical change of spirit in the Roman people. The Romans had entered the war reluctantly. There are indications that now the people were at first somewhat reluctant to make peace. Polybius tells us [2] that they rejected the terms made by Lutatius and sent

[1] de Sanctis, *Storia dei Romani*, iii. 192.

[2] Polyb. i. 63.

commissioners to examine the situation before they assented. They had the self-consciousness of a power which had 'arrived', and had tasted the sweets of foreign conquest. This had been the first testing of the new union of Italy in the furnace of war, and the Confederation had stood the test.

In the second war with Carthage, which began some twenty years later, the Confederation had to bear a heavier strain. Before this new struggle opened, the genius of Hamilcar had laid the foundations of a new Punic power in Spain. He belonged to a famous family, the house of Barca or Barak, which played a great part in the imperial history of Carthage. The conquered land after seven years under Hasdrubal was handed on to Hamilcar's more famous son Hannibal, the greatest commander with whom the Romans ever had to contend.

But before their long seventeen years' conflict with him began they had to confirm their position in Italy. In the first place they had to suppress several risings of the Celtic population of the north and this led to the extension of Roman power into the valley of the Po. Secondly, they had to deal with the pirate power of Illyria on the Dalmatian coast and assert their mastery over the Adriatic. This was immensely significant, because it was the first decisive step in that eastern advance of Rome which ended in her taking over the defence of the Greek world and of Hellenism in general against the forces of Northern Europe and of the Eastern peoples. The supremacy over the Celtic peoples in Italy was not achieved without great slaughter: 40,000 Gauls are said to have fallen at the final engagement at Telamon in Etruria in 225. The completion of the conquest was marked by the distribution of land allotments (232) and by the building of the great north road (220), the Via Flaminia already mentioned. About the same time in 218 were founded the two Latin colonies of Placentia and Cremona. These famous towns command the passage of the Po, and the meeting-point of the great lines of communication which connect Rome and Italy by land with the rest of the world. For from this commanding centre in the Po valley the roads go east, west, and north, to Gaul, and Germany and the Balkan Peninsula.[1] Rome, then, was rapidly becoming the centre of the Mediterranean world, but the position was still precarious. Carthage still barred the way.

The invasion of Italy by Hannibal was one of the boldest ventures in history, and it was played for a great stake, the command of the Mediterranean world. It was unexpected, because the Romans never imagined that Hannibal would dare to push on so far from his base at New Carthage in Spain and would isolate himself in a foreign country, while the Roman navy had complete command of the sea. The rapidity of Hannibal's march and the miscalculation of the Romans gave him a firm footing in Italy, which with amazing skill he managed to retain for fourteen years. His successful skirmish on the Ticinus and the battle on the Trebia followed by his great victories first at the Trasimene Lake (217) in Etruria and then at Cannae (216) near the Aufidus in Apulia, shook the Roman supremacy in Italy to its foundations. Two things saved it: the dogged patience and persistence of the Roman character, and the loyalty of the Allies.

It was not for nothing that Rome had based her Italian policy on generous principles. There were indeed some backsliders among the Italians. After the great disaster at Cannae in 216, Capua (the Campanian city on the Volturno, which the traveller still passes through on the way to Naples)

[1] For Roman roads see Prof. Stuart Jones, *Companion to Roman History*, pp. 40 ff.

and the Samnites and Lucanians joined the invader, but even in this searching time of trial most of the Greek towns of the south remained faithful. In 209 twelve out of thirty Latin colonies were obliged to refuse men and money from sheer exhaustion, but the northern colonies stood firm, and in the end the Italian Confederation completely justified itself. Never did a policy of wise incorporation win a greater success.

The fighting was not in one country alone. Throughout the war the Romans had fighting on hand in Spain as well as in Italy. For this they had the great advantage over Carthage that they could transport their troops by sea through their supreme sea-power; but the Carthaginian resistance was serious, and Rome's powers were strained to the utmost by the great defeat of 212 in Spain, in which two Roman commanders, Publius and Cornelius Scipio, were killed and a great army was destroyed. But the next year brought relief, for in Italy the Roman spirits were raised by the reduction of the rebellious city of Capua, while the younger P. Cornelius Scipio, a commander-in-chief of only twenty-four years, began to retrieve the Roman fortunes in Spain. But the Carthaginian resistance was not exhausted. Hannibal's brother Hasdrubal was able to make his way to Italy with an army to relieve his hard-pressed brother, but his defeat at the Metaurus [1] in 207 marked the last crisis in the war within the peninsula. The closing scenes of the drama of war were enacted in Africa, where the young Scipio dealt the final blow at Zama, 202, a battle which ended the power of Carthage for ever.

The result of this, the second Punic war, was to convert

[1] By a subtle stroke of flattery Horace uses this victory, in which C. Claudius Nero bore a part, to glorify Augustus and his two stepsons, Tiberius, afterwards emperor, and Nero Claudius Drusus, the conqueror of Rhaetia and the Alps. Horace, *Odes*, iv. 4.

Carthage from a great Mediterranean State into a mere town, to make Rome supreme in the Western Mediterranean lands, and almost at once to add Spain to her subject territory. This meant the formation of two new provinces, Nearer and Further Spain, for Spain was too large for one governor. It also meant what was more serious, the inauguration of practically permanent military service: for the new territory had to be secured by a large garrison of Roman troops. From this time forward Spain was not indeed conquered, but the foundations were laid of a provincial life which became intensely Roman, and supplied, in the end, men of letters, administrators, and even emperors to Rome.

Another great change had been effected. Even in earlier days, when military necessity arose, the Roman government had extended the Imperium of its consuls; but with the Younger Scipio for the first time we find military command prolonged over a period of years. It is significant that the admiring Spaniards offered him the kingship of their country.[1] This was an ominous sign that Roman imperial policy had brought with it the menace of a military monarchy.

The Punic danger was gone. But across the Adriatic Rome had to deal with Macedon and with the States of Greece. Through all the vicissitudes of the war with Hannibal Rome had not only to fight in Italy and Spain, but to play her part as a European power coming for the first time in contact with the Greek world of the East. Philip of Macedon's alliance with Hannibal in 215 inevitably involved the Romans in the politics of the Greek world. It was Rome's good fortune that at this time her old alliance with Egypt could be renewed. That alliance served as a counterpoise against Macedonian influence in the Mediterranean. Rome's diplomacy was now directed

[1] Polybius, x. 40.

to securing a coalition of Pergamum and other Greek States against Philip, which should prevent him from active intervention on the side of Carthage. Throughout the period of foreign conquest with which we are now concerned we can trace the same policy: friendship and alliance with those leading States of Greece which were still independent—Pergamum, Rhodes, the Aetolian League—passing, as Rome's power grew and one enemy after another was conquered, from friendship into vassalage and from vassalage into absolute conquest and absorption. The same policy was pursued in Africa, where the Romans for two centuries maintained relations with client princes in Numidia and Mauretania. With the help of these princes they were enabled first to crush Carthage and later to protect the borders of the Roman Empire from the wild tribes of the desert.

The power of Macedon had effected nothing in the Punic wars, but it was still a menace to Rome, for Philip had made a compact with Antiochus, the Seleucid king of Syria, for the partition of Egypt, and this meant nothing less than that Rome would find the Eastern world closed to her commerce and her influence unless Philip could be crushed. The second Punic War was hardly over when Rome found a cause of quarrel with Philip, and with the help of her Greek allies—Rhodes and Pergamum—reduced him by the battle of Cynoscephalae in 198 to the position of a second-rate power. The conflict proved conclusively that the Roman legion, developed from its original solid mass-formation into the more elastic manipular system, was more than a match for the armies of the Greek East, with their inferior discipline and vigour.

This victory over Macedon left Rome the dominating power in the southern part of the Balkan Peninsula. She now became the acknowledged patron of the freedom of Hellas, which was publicly proclaimed by Flamininus at the Isthmian Games of 194. But that freedom was still threatened by Antiochus the Seleucid, the king of Syria, one of the kingdoms carved out of Alexandria's Empire. The position of Rome as the patron and protector of the Greek States remained precarious until Antiochus the Great was defeated by L. Scipio at Magnesia, 190. This battle decided for the time the fate of the Hellenic East. Syria ceased to be a formidable power and was kept to the east of Mt. Taurus, and Rome acquired that decisive influence over Asia Minor which, though threatened more than once by Mithradates of Pontus and later by the Parthians, was never completely lost until the Turks overwhelmed the last remnant of Rome's empire in the East. But Rome's conquest of the Balkan Peninsula was not complete until she had defeated Philip's successor Perseus on the field of Pydna and broken up the once proud monarchy of Macedon into four Republican Leagues, 167. The final step was taken by the conversion of Macedonia into a Province twenty years later, into which Achaea, which comprised the ancient Greek States, was absorbed.

The year 146 was a decisive year. The destruction in that year not only of Corinth, the commercial capital of Greece, but also of Carthage, Rome's other great trade rival, marked the changed spirit of Rome. She had used her victories to break her commercial rivals in the Mediterranean. The further outcome of Rome's victory on the Greek mainland was that the States of Pergamum and Rhodes, having been used as allies and friends against Syria and Macedon, were now shorn of all influence and reduced to complete dependence. In the same year with the victory of Pydna, 168, Antiochus Epiphanes, the Seleucid king who had grown up in Rome,[1] was

[1] Bevan, *House of Seleucus*, ii. 128.

made to withdraw from Alexandria, and Egypt accepted once for all the protectorate of Rome. Thus, with her great trade rivals crushed and the richest country on the Mediterranean seaboard reduced to vassalage, Rome was able henceforward to extend her trade unhindered over the whole known world.

But these successive victories meant that the Romans had undertaken new and heavy responsibilities. By the conquest of Macedon they became the guardians of the Balkan Peninsula against the moving peoples of Central Europe. From generation to generation they had to deal, in a succession of irregular campaigns, with the wild tribes of the region of the Danube until something like a scientific frontier was established by the first Roman Emperor, Augustus. One of that Emperor's greatest tasks was to knit up the defences of the north and to construct the outline of a defensive frontier policy against Germans, Sarmatians, and Dacians, which was consolidated in the course of a century by his successors. This was a later work; but its ultimate achievement was a duty which now fell upon Rome, if her position in the lands east of the Adriatic was to be maintained. Not only so, but the warning given to Antiochus Epiphanes, when Popilius in 168 drew a circle round him and made him obey the Roman bidding [1] and retire from Egypt, carried with it, for those who could look forward, the fateful consequence that in Asia and Egypt, no less than in Europe, the Romans would sooner or later become the defenders of Hellenism against the Oriental world. For the present they were content to exercise influence in the East by diplomacy. They had still much to do in Italy itself before they could undertake further responsibilities outside.

The Italian Allies, we have seen, had in the main been faithful to Rome in the war with Hannibal: the colonies were staunch,

[1] Polyb. xxix. 27.

Tivoli (Tibur) from the west, by Edward Lear.

and the Umbrian and Sabellian races were becoming merged in the Roman unity, but the Celtic tribes, which had supported Hannibal, were still unsettled, and the war with Carthage was hardly over when Rome had to deal with risings in the north, of Boii, Insubres, and Cenomani in the region of the Padus, where it will be remembered Roman colonization had already been active before Hannibal's invasion. This was the last expiring effort of the Celtic tribes, and it ended, as it was bound to end, in their subjection and in the rapid Romanization of their country. The new roads, the Via Flaminia already mentioned by anticipation and the Via Aemilia, which has given its name to a province of Italy to-day, confirmed the Roman hold on the country. From this time dates the final consolidation of the Celtic region. It was secured by these roads and by the colonies founded upon the Via Aemilia, together with those like Placentia and Cremona on the Po, dating back to 218, and Aquileia, 181, in the north-east, on the highway to the Balkan region, the last Latin colony in Italy. This Celtic district was, it would seem, for the time administered not by regular provincial governors, but as a part of Italy, under the consuls or other Roman officers. It was only by Sulla that Gallia Cisalpina was made a province, to remain so for forty years until Augustus finally unified the Italian Peninsula, and divided it into eleven districts (*regiones*), corresponding roughly to the earlier racial divisions.

The same policy of consolidation by colonies was applied to the centre and the south—Etruria, Picenum (183), Campania, Apulia, Lucania, and Bruttium. Here the normal development by means of town foundations was followed: in the Celtic country beyond the Po something of the canton system still remained until the end of the Republic. The Celtic wars were further complicated by the forty years of petty warfare with their neighbours, the Ligurians of the Riviera, who were persistent and troublesome fighters, and who were not finally conquered till about 165. Their subdual made it possible to develop the coast-road north-westward to Massilia, the Roman ally in Southern Gaul who provided the half-way house for Romans travelling to the Spanish provinces. The Aurelian road to Lucca and the cross-road from Lucca to Arretium probably belong to this period. They are all part of the great work of Romanization in Italy.

If we look at the state of Italy thus united under Rome and compare it with that of 120 years earlier, several features strike us. First, the process of Romanization has made a steady advance, although, even now, the unity of the peninsula was not complete. Secondly, there is a hardening in the Romans' attitude to their allies. The freedom of migration was being curtailed. In 187 some 12,000 Latins were expelled from Rome, and ten years later a Claudian law enacted a further ejection of allies from the capital. At the same time the ranks of the citizen body were more strictly closed, and access to the citizenship became more difficult for Italian communities and individuals. There is one fact of great significance which illustrates the changed relations between Rome and her Allies. Down to 181 B.C. when Aquileia, the last Latin colony, was founded in Italy, Latin colonies in Italy were as frequent as the colonies of Roman citizens. After that date only Roman colonies, i.e. colonies with full citizenship, were founded in Italy. The reason was that while in the earlier period Roman citizens were content to waive their citizen rights in order to receive an allotment in a Latin colony, the position of the Latins now was thought inferior, and the colonists would not consent to go as settlers unless they received the full Roman rights. Livy, writing under Augustus, but doubtless basing his story on good authority, tells us that a consul of 173 B.C., L. Postumius, who was journeying southwards on the public service, took a new departure. He called on Praeneste, an allied city on his road, to give him supplies for his journey. 'Till that day', says Livy, 'no Roman had ever been a burden or expense to the allies in any matter.'[1] These words bear a striking testimony to the virtues of the earlier Republic; but they are also a warning sign that the spirit of the governing class of Rome was beginning to degenerate. The result was that eighty years later they had to pay for their short-sighted policy by a war which laid waste huge tracts of Italy and greatly advanced the economic decline of the peninsula.

This crowded hundred years of Roman history is the great century of the Roman Republic, in which step by step the rule of the Romans was extended on all sides until they became the supreme power in the Mediterranean. It is also the age of Senatorial government at its best and strongest. Many reasons combined to consolidate the power of the Senate.

(1) The Assemblies of citizens, the *Comitia* and the *Concilium Plebis*, were bound to become weaker just in proportion as the arms of Rome advanced. The Romans, like the Greeks, had no idea of what we call 'representation'. Their Assemblies consisted of all full citizens, not of certain citizens selected to represent the rest. In early days when Rome meant only the city and the surrounding district of Latium all citizens could take a personal share in government. As soon as the bounds of the franchise were enlarged, it became clear that the more distant citizens could but rarely exercise their active rights: they might come once a year to Rome for an election or a festival, but only those who happened to reside in or near

[1] 'Ante hunc consulem nemo unquam sociis in ulla re oneri aut sumptui fuit.' Liv. xlii. 1.

Rome could take part in the day-to-day or week-to-week duties of normal government. Further, the very nature and constitution of the Assemblies limited their powers. They could simply say 'yes' or 'no' to the proposals laid before them. They had no power to amend, and without such power no assembly can be strong. The Senate, which drafted the bills put before the people, was, on the other hand, a real deliberative body, with free power to discuss and amend. Clearly the control was bound to rest with the smaller body, the Senate.

(2) The Magistrates of Rome were *annual*, and, further, each magistrate was one of a group whose members were all of equal power and could interfere with one another at every stage. The result of this, the collegiate principle, was that no single magistrate could stand alone, and that the power of the executive depended entirely on the backing of the Senate, the body from which the magistrates came and into which they returned.

(3) The Magistrates of Rome, like those of Athens before Pericles, were unpaid, and there was no permanent civil service to carry on the daily routine of government. This being so, the current duties of government naturally tended to fall more and more on the Senate, which was composed of ex-magistrates of tried experience. The Senators, being resident in Rome and well-to-do, could give daily attention to current business and deal with the multitude of questions to which the government of Rome and Italy and the provinces gave rise, without reference to the sovereign assembly of citizens. We have only to read Livy's history to see how by a process as inevitable as it was advantageous, the conduct of affairs passed completely into the hands of the Senate. The affairs of Italy, e.g. the arrangements for founding or replenishing or fortifying colonies, and

for protecting or punishing Allies; the ordering of conquered territories abroad, the government of them when organized; the direction of the armies of the State; the conduct of diplomacy and the making of war and peace; and finally the control of finance—all these varied powers and duties which make up the sum of what we call government, were in their hands. It was with good reason that in official documents the Senate's name stands first—S.P.Q.R., *Senatus Populusque Romanus*—the Senate and People of Rome.

And in these years the Senate fulfilled its duties well. The original narrow circle of the Patriciate no longer controlled affairs. The mixed nobility of officers, drawn from both patrician and plebeian homes, and supplied not only from Rome and Latium but from many Italian towns, had become consolidated into a compact society in which governing capacity and a strong sense of service produced a high average level of ability. From year to year Consuls and Praetors were found to lead the armies of Rome and administer justice to citizens and foreigners. This high average of capacity is not hard to account for. The avenue to the Senate was the Magistracy; but to this few but the sons of Senators could hope to attain. The principle of heredity—the idea of son following father—was strong at Rome. But there was no rigid rule of succession, and, far more important, there was no preference of the eldest son. It was this basis of heredity tempered by selection which gave to the Senate its immense capacity and power. In one region in particular we must note its activity: in the development of law. For it was in this period that Roman law took a great step forward. In 243 the judicial duties of Rome were for the first time divided between two officers—a City Praetor to give justice to citizens, and a Foreign Praetor to give justice as between citizens and foreigners. From the annual activities of these Praetors there was gradually developed a system of law which came to be one of the chief glories of the Roman State. From the judgements given in these courts there grew up a body of case law, which, codified later by the lawyers of the Empire, became the foundation of a large part of the law of Europe. And as time went on, and the growth of Rome was extended over peoples who had legal ideas and institutions of their own the wider principles of the *ius gentium*, the law common to nations, occupied an increasingly large place in Roman legal practice, reacted on the whole legal system of Rome and supplied equitable principles of expansion which a purely traditional system would have lacked. How much Roman law owed in its origin and development to Greece is a question not here to be discussed, but throughout Roman history the growth of law and its adaptation to an ever-widening multitude of conditions is vastly important and is a side of the history which we are apt to overlook. For some seven hundred years much of the best intellect of Rome was directed to building up the great structure which found its consummation in the Codes of Theodosius and Justinian. Here we have only to note the significance of Roman law and to remind ourselves that it is the perpetual correlative of Roman conquest and Roman rule, an abiding and developing element throughout Rome's history.

Two more things must be mentioned: first, the development of Roman literature; second, the spirit of the Roman army.

It was in the year after the first Punic War ended that the first play of Livius Andronicus, a prisoner of war from Tarentum, was produced on a Roman stage. He was soon followed by Cn. Naevius, a Latin, born in Campania, who was the first to lead the way in distinctively Roman drama and epic. Plautus, the Umbrian (254–184), in the same age produced a quantity of Latin comedies translated from the Greek. But the greatest name of the period is that of Q. Ennius, the Calabrian, whose tragedies and whose epic of Roman history, the *Annales*, were the first great Latin works of literature. It was Ennius who in his epic substituted the hexameter for the old native Saturnian metre, and paved the way for the great achievements of Lucretius and Virgil.

Two general remarks may be made on this literary development:

(1) It was founded on Greek models and largely dependent on Greek literature for subject and material.

(2) From the first it was Italian rather than purely Roman. In literature as in political and military strength the greatness of Rome depended on her control and co-ordination of the spiritual and material resources of the whole peninsula.

> Tantae molis erat Romanam condere gentem.[1]
> Such pains it cost to build the Roman State.

The Army. The great work accomplished by Rome in these years could not have been achieved without her citizen army. Without going into details, it may be worth while to notice one or two points:

(1) The army was a citizen army; all citizens of a certain property were liable to service from seventeen to forty-six.

(2) Rome's wars with the Italian peoples had improved her arms and had adapted the heavy phalanx system to a more elastic formation.

(3) The troops were officered by the nobility of Rome—the Consuls and sometimes the Praetors of the year, and below them the tribunes of the soldiers who were the legionary officers. But the backbone of the army was supplied by the Centurions, whose service was more continuous and who by

[1] Virg. *Aen.* i. 33.

their mastery of drill and discipline held the companies together and provided the permanent tradition of the service.

(4) Side by side with the legions (as we have seen) served the cohorts and squadrons of the Allies, in their own formations but under Roman officers, prefects of the Allies (*praefecti sociorum*).

What the spirit of the Centurion was may best be seen from a speech given us by Livy in an account of a protest made by some centurions in 171 at being posted to commands lower than those that they had held before.[1]

'I Spurius Ligustinus of the Crustumine tribe was born in the Sabine country. My father left me an acre of land and a little cottage in which I was born and brought up and I live there still. As soon as I was old enough my father gave me his niece in marriage, who brought as her dowry her free birth, her good name, and fruitfulness that would do honour to a richer home. We have six sons and two daughters, both now married: four sons are of age, two still boys. I entered the army in the consulship of P. Sulpicius and C. Aurelius [200 B.C.]. I fought in the ranks two years in the army that crossed to Macedonia to fight against Philip: in the third year I was made centurion of the 10th maniple of the *Hastati*,[2] as the reward of merit. Discharged after the conquest of Macedon I served as a volunteer with M. Porcius Cato in Spain—there could be no severer critic of valour, as all would admit—and he promoted me to the 1st maniple. I served the third time as a volunteer in the war against the Aetolians and Antiochus and was promoted to the leading maniple of the *Principes*. Later I served on two annual campaigns. Next I served in two campaigns in

[1] Liv. xlii. 34, slightly abbreviated.

[2] *Hastati*, *Principes*, and *Triarii* were the three main divisions of the Roman infantry, in ascending order of rank. The centurion of the first maniple of the Triarii was called *Primipilus*.

Spain and for four years was centurion of the first maniple of the legion. I have been honoured 34 times by my officers and had six civic crowns.

'I have served 22 campaigns and am over 50. But in no circumstances am I going to beg off service if I am thought fit, and am prepared to accept any rank to which I am assigned by the Tribunes. I shall always take pains to surpass all others in valour, as my comrades will agree I have always done. And I advise all you my comrades like me to put yourselves at the disposal of the Senate and to consider any post as honourable, where you can defend the Roman Commonwealth.'

It is not surprising that an army of tough material, so officered, should have done what it did.

3

The Decline of Senatorial Government and the Period of Revolution

We have seen how a single city state of central Italy had mastered the peninsula and now dictated policies to the Eastern and the Western world. The next 160 years saw the extension of Roman conquest carried still further, and the penetration of Italy by Roman ideas and government made more complete. But the outward expansion of the Empire is in contrast with the declining moral of the governing class. The best men of that class made attempts to reform the body politic; but their order, the nobles as a body, were unsympathetic, and the citizens at large showed no proper appreciation of the claims of the Italians outside the franchise. The result was that the conflict for the franchise ended in a devastating Italian war which left a permanent mark on Italy. The attempts at reform led to revolution and civil war. The struggle became one between rival military leaders. The victory of Julius Caesar led to a short period of masterful rule and activity, in which the main lines were traced of the monarchy to come. Caesar worked with a bold hand which paid no regard to immemorial convention or to the feelings of the Senatorial order, and his murder not unnaturally followed. That is the tragedy which Shakespeare has made familiar to us all. It was the irony of the conflict that his death led not to a Republican restoration such as Brutus dreamed of, but to a bloody and prolonged series of civil wars which ended only with the battle of Actium, and led to the establishment of the Principate, the government of one man under Republican forms.

We have now to trace the main features of this stormy time. We have to piece them together from fragmentary sources until we come to the life-time of Cicero and Caesar, when we are fortunate enough to have contemporary letters and speeches and above all the commentaries of Caesar, his own story of the conquest of Gaul and of the Civil War. With the death of Cicero we are again reduced mainly to secondary sources for the closing years of the Republic and the final conflicts between the heirs of Caesar's power.

We have hitherto been mainly concerned with the outward expansion of the Roman State. We cannot understand this last stage in the history of the Republic without reviewing the social and economic conditions in Italy. The basis of Roman life had been the land. It was on the peasant-farmers of the expanding Roman State that Rome relied for her armies. But this farming class had been affected in two ways by the past two centuries of war. Service in the field had taken many men away from their farms; the actual loss of life had been considerable; and finally the transmarine wars had brought large numbers of slaves into Italy, whose labour tended to introduce a new phase of agriculture—the system of working the land by gangs of slaves. With the extension of conquest in Italy Rome had acquired large tracts of land for the State : this had been disposed of partly in small lots, granted in full ownership to citizens or allies ; partly in large tracts granted in occupation, without ownership, for pasture (*scripturarius ager*) or for agriculture to squatters (*possessores*) whose holdings, though not freeholds, could be transferred like property. The effect of the great wars had been to diminish the small holdings and to encourage the encroachment of the large holders, while the introduction of large-scale farming on the Carthaginian model and the abundance of slaves, encouraged the growth of large estates (*latifundia*), worked by slave labour.

At the same time a new capitalist class had come into existence, partly as a consequence of the fortunes made in war contracts, partly from the extension of Roman trade beyond the seas. This class found a sphere for its activities not only in extended commerce but also as we saw in the financial arrangements connected with the taxation of the provinces. The financial system of the Roman Republic still remained simple. The annual system of magistracy meant that the Quaestors, who were the financial officers of the State, gained no continuous experience, and in the absence of a permanent civil service to conduct and control finance, a large part of the revenues of Rome was handled by the companies of public contractors who made their bargains with the State for fixed periods and under the State acted as collectors of revenue. This system relieved the Government of the necessity of having a developed Treasury system, and was an almost necessary result of the Senatorial ideal of government which was founded on *the unpaid services of an aristocracy*. But the system had the dangerous result that it produced a class of very rich men, outside the ranks of the Senate, exercising immense indirect influence, but, from their exclusion from the Senate, bearing no direct responsibility for public policy or for the conduct of affairs. At the same time the richer Senatorial families, who were excluded from commerce, were putting into the land the capital which they had gained by foreign wars, with the natural result that the tendency to crush out the small holders was increased. The attraction of men from Italian towns to the city of Rome had collected there a large population of comparatively idle citizens, some of them engaged in the service of the rich and in the exercise of crafts; but the majority of them becoming more and more mere spectators of the daily life and amusements of the capital, 'the dregs of Romulus,'[1] as Cicero calls them. The households of Italy had in the past been in the main self-supporting: they had manufactured their own clothes and provided for their own necessities. Life had been simple and the household self-sufficing. The growth of wealth and luxury had created new needs, which were supplied largely by importation from the highly organized manufacturing centres of Asia and Egypt, which poured their products into Italy through Puteoli and other ports, partly by the labour of slaves and freedmen. In Rome and Italy as elsewhere slave labour had made trade and craftsmanship come to be regarded as sordid and illiberal.

The new world which thus confronts us had its nobler aspects. The closer contact with Greece had brought new interests and new motives into Roman life. Already, as we saw, the Greek influences in the Italian peninsula itself had given rise to the beginnings of comedy with Plautus and of epic with Ennius, but with the conquest of Macedonia and Achaea the full flood of Greek influence came to pervade the life of the Senatorial nobles, in spite of the protest of certain old-fashioned spirits which suspected the new learning. The later Greek philosophic schools—the Academy, the Stoics, the Epicureans—

[1] *In Romuli faece*, Cic. *Epp. ad Att.*, 2. 1. 8.

and the political principles of the Greek statesmen of the Achaean League, the wealth of Greek literature as a whole, from Homer to the schools of Alexandria—all these came in to exercise their potent forces. Higher education became Graeco-Roman—the outlook of the educated class was widened, and the better men of Rome found in Greek ideals of literature and political life a new stimulus and a new food for their spiritual life. But it was part of the tragedy of Roman history that these new influences came into Roman life at a time when the political and social problems had become almost overwhelming, and so the choice spirits, like the Gracchi, who had drunk of the Greek springs of political wisdom, were foredoomed to failure in their attempt to re-create or renew the Republic of Rome. The enrichment of Roman life was to be seen in the next hundred years of Roman literature, in Lucretius with his austere and passionate union of science with imagination, in Catullus with his lyric power and passion, in Horace with his happy mingling of humanity and worldly wisdom. And finally the great works of Virgil, his *Aeneid* and *Georgics* written in

> ' the stateliest measure
> Ever moulded by the lips of man,'

were the product of North Italian genius expressing the ideals of Italian country life and Roman government in a form based on a Greek model, but in its character individual, national, and supreme in its appeal. But all these poets and the great names in prose—Cicero, Livy, Tacitus—belong to the age when government was passing or had passed already from the hands of a free Republic to the control of a single ruler.

The success of Rome in the earlier age had rested on character: on the family life and discipline, with its simplicity, severity, and efficiency. The new influences had broken into this simple life, and the new generation which was growing up in Rome was

Licenza and the Hills round Horace's Farm, by Edward Lear.

much more complex and had much harder problems to settle than merely conquering mountain tribes or expelling a foreign invader from Italy.

Two main problems confronted the new age: (1) the government of Italy and its social regeneration; (2) the government of the transmarine possessions—which now extended eastward to the Taurus, and westward to Spain.

The political efforts and achievements of the brothers Tiberius and Gaius Gracchus, which open the political experiments of the new age, give an indication of the needs of the time and a forecast of the hopelessness of the problems to be solved. They were partly social and economical, partly political. The attempt of the two brothers to restore or to enlarge the class of small farmers had some success, but could achieve comparatively little in face of the fact that corn-growing, though it might support the farmer and his household, was not a paying industry on a large scale. The vine and the olive were, indeed, becoming much more the staple product of the country,[1] and were grown with profit; but there were other factors which prevented any substantial revival of farming at this time: the continuance of foreign wars, the revolt of the Allies, and the succession of civil wars which occupied a large part of the last fifty years of the Republic. Later attempts were made at land legislation—by Sulla and Julius Caesar, but they were legislating not so much for the landless farmer as for the retired soldier, who, coming to the land without experience, was often an unsatisfactory landholder and had to give up his new profession and fall back into the ranks of the idle or disorderly class.[2]

[1] See Prof. Stuart Jones, op. cit., pp. 308 ff. Cf. Ferrero, *Greatness and Decline of Rome*, i. p. 49. On the whole land question Mr. Heitland's *Agricola* supplies abundant information.

[2] Cf. Sallust, *Cat.*, ch. 16, 28.

If we try to sum up the results of the agrarian legislation of this period, we come to the conclusion that far more was done by civil war to destroy agricultural prosperity than by any political measures to restore it. It was not till the peace of Augustus gave Italy tranquillity and a revival of rural and municipal life that Italian agriculture achieved any real improvement. The land was the foundation of the old Italian life, and the problem of its distribution had exercised men's minds for generations: the historians tell us that a Licinian law as early as 367 B.C. had limited the size of single holdings of the *Public Land* and that the law of Gracchus was only a reinforcement of the old limit. However this may be, the event proved that the magic of property was not strong enough to fight against the attraction of Rome and the decline in the free population. Nevertheless we must not suppose that small farms wholly disappeared. Till the end of the first century A.D. many holdings of moderate size survived, and the *latifundia*, the wide estates worked by slaves, which the historians deplore, were in this age at least only prevalent in certain regions—in parts of Etruria and Campania and other regions where the conditions favoured pasturage or agriculture on a large scale.[1]

At the best then the land-laws of the Gracchi were only a qualified success. From the *constitutional* point of view their legislation had fatal consequences. How was it that two of the most generous and gifted statesmen of the governing nobility failed and met their death in their attempts at reform?

The Tribunate, which they made use of for their legislation, had been in origin a popular office, but the extension of Roman citizenship, as we have seen, had made the citizen assemblies unreal, and thrown all the power of the constitution into the hands of the Senate. The Tribunes, like the regular magis-

[1] Mommsen, *Die italische Bodentheilung und die Alimentartafeln* (*Historische Schriften*, ii, p. 123).

trates, were drawn from the official nobility, and shared in general the prejudices of their order. The consequence was that the Tribunate had lost its democratic associations, and by a perfectly natural development had become only a wheel in the Senatorial machine, and the plebeian assembly over which they presided, and which possessed legislative power since 287, had come completely under Senatorial control. Thus, when the Gracchi revived the old ideal of the Tribunate, as an independent instrument of reform, they came into collision with Senatorial usage, the strongest force at Rome, and when Tiberius Gracchus went further and deposed his colleague, the tribune Octavius, for vetoing his act, he struck a heavy blow at constitutional government. Two things came out clearly from the fate of the Gracchi: first, that it was futile to attempt to rule through the popular assembly; the Assembly could never be made a useful instrument of government. Secondly, that no reform could be effective which did not widen the composition and change the character of the Senate.

The younger brother Gaius Gracchus struck out in two new directions, which were significant of the future. Instead of widening the basis of the Senate and bringing into it new blood from the Italian towns, as had happened in earlier days, he constituted a new order in the State in the so-called *Equites* or Knights, by giving to the rich capitalists a new prestige and the privilege of serving on juries and collecting the taxes of Asia. The result was on the whole calamitous. The new order had vast influence, direct and indirect, but none of the responsibilities of government, and as a class it developed no public spirit. Its interest in making money out of the taxes of Asia made it a mischievous element in politics, equally dangerous whether it acted in league with corrupt governors, or used its power to procure the recall or condemnation of just ones. As a substantial moneyed class they gave a certain stability to any government they supported, but they brought no new or quickening idea into Roman life or administration. It was only when a century later Augustus remodelled the Order and brought it under disciplined control that it became a serviceable element in the State. In the meantime it had done nothing for the cause of free government.

The Gracchi had legislated by direct appeal to the Assembly, but though they certainly sympathized with the claims of the Italians outside the citizen body they did not succeed in achieving their inclusion, urgent as the claim was and vital for the security of Italy. The Allies, though they had shed their blood in the foreign wars out of proportion to their numbers and in excess of their treaty obligations, were still refused access to the full franchise. This exclusion was felt the more because during the last hundred years Italy was becoming in language, manners, and form of government more completely Roman. The Roman type of government with its two chief magistrates and its Senate was becoming widely spread, and the Latin language and Roman law were being widely adopted. The Italians were fighting Rome's battles and were travelling far and wide under the Roman flag, to engage in business in Asia and Africa, Gaul and Spain. There was no reason for their exclusion from the citizen body but the selfishness of the existing citizens. The wiser statesmen saw this and proposed inclusion, and the rejection of this policy led to the devastating Social war, which turned Italy upside down for two years. The laws which followed the conclusion of the war converted all Italy south of the Po into Roman territory, and gave Latin rights to the country between the Po and the Alps—rights which were converted into full Roman citizenship by Julius Caesar in 49 B.C.

The legislation of the Gracchi showed once for all that the Comitia could not govern: legislation by the people meant legislation by the mob of Rome. Their reforming successor, the great Livius Drusus, had in some ways a wider outlook: his idea of a widened Senate was sound and constructive; but his plans were wrecked when he tried to satisfy Italians as well as Roman citizens. He fell because he was a good Italian as well as a good Roman. The revolt of the Allies which followed, the Social or, as it is sometimes called, the Marsian War, achieved his Italian aims. Italy became Roman up to the Po, but it was an Italy impoverished by war.

The question of distribution of the new citizens after the Social war for voting purposes gave some trouble, but was finally settled in a generous sense. But before this unification of Italy was completed, Rome had experienced the danger and the responsibility of her position in Europe as the guardian of Latin and Hellenic culture: the threatening of invasion from the barbarians of the North, Celts and Teutons, was a renewal of the Celtic peril of three centuries earlier. For the moment it was crushed by Marius, the people's general, but it was not till Julius Caesar had conquered Gaul and Augustus had created something like a scientific frontier on Rhine and Danube that the danger was fully averted. Throughout this age the Northern peril loomed large in the background of Roman life.

But the crisis brought with it another danger, as ominous to Roman liberty as the Northern peril was to the existence of the Roman State. The renewed consulships of Marius, re-elected consul again and again in order to meet dangerous enemies of Rome in Africa and in the North, emphasized what was becoming an immediate danger to the Republic—the danger of the omnipotence of a powerful military commander. It was a grave defect of the Roman constitution that it did not separate civil and military command, and that the armies of the State were controlled by the consuls of the year, who were also responsible for the conduct of civil affairs. True, the prolongation of foreign wars had already been leading to an adjustment by which the command (*imperium*) was prolonged for military purposes beyond the consular year of office, and thus military was getting to be separated from civil rule ; but even so the high prestige of a proconsul or a propraetor at the head of a victorious army was destined to become an imminent danger when a generation of Senators grew up who had lost the good tradition of discipline and civil obedience. Military command thus became an object of competition among the nobles, and the military leader became a determining force in politics. This menace of domination by military leaders haunts the whole of the last century of the Republic. And the danger of military rule did not come merely from without. It was becoming almost a necessity if laws were to be carried in the now disordered state of the constitution.

The failure of the mob of Rome to protect the Gracchi was a sign that no legislator in the future could appeal to the Assembly with success unless he had an army which he could call to his support. The armies of Marius, Sulla, Pompey, and Caesar in succession were the means by which the laws of this period were carried. Each of these military leaders was brought to the front by the opportunities or needs of foreign war. Marius put an end to a lingering war in Africa, where Roman merchants and colonists had suffered from the incompetence of senatorial commanders, and he had checked the invaders from the North : Sulla had fought and conquered Mithradates, the last great enemy of Rome in Asia. Pompey and Caesar we shall consider later. This dominance of the great generals was largely due to the fact that the army from Marius's time became practically professional—open to all classes, and not as in earlier days restricted to men who owned land and had a stake in the country. It was natural that such an army should be ready to sacrifice loyalty towards the State to personal allegiance to a general. It is one of the most striking ironies in Roman history that Sulla, the one statesman who posed as the guardian of Senatorial government and of the old order, was the first to invade Rome with a Roman army (in 88). That act and the organized butchery of his Proscriptions when he became absolute ruler were fatal precedents which were only too faithfully followed.

Italy had already suffered much since the Social War from the conflicts between the armies of Marius and of Sulla, and the massacres enacted by the Marian party; and this final revenge of Sulla on his enemies still further weakened the resources of the State, not to speak of the terrible example which it left. The bloodshed might have been a price worth paying had it ended in a broad and stable government. As it was, it made only a momentary pause. Sulla was a typical Senator and could see no further than the rest of his order. His legislation, except for his reorganization of the criminal law, which was a business-like and efficient piece of work, was in the main reactionary and worse than useless.[1] It was an attempt to establish the power of the Senate on a statutory instead of a customary basis. To do this he destroyed the power of the Tribunes by making the Tribunate a bar to higher office and by requiring the sanction of the Senate for all laws of the plebeian assembly. At the same time by his revival of the laws regulating the tenure of magistracies, and his reorganization of the relation of home and foreign command, he tried to reinforce the two main principles of Senatorial government: (1) the principle that no one but Senators should rule; (2) the principle that no Senator should

[1] Sulla's replenishment of the ranks of the Senate may seem an exception. But it is not clear that he brought it into any closer relation to Italian life or introduced any valuable elements. See Greenidge and Clay, *Sources for Roman History*, p. 173.

have more than his share of office, and that all military command should be controlled by the Senate. Sulla's degradation of the Equestrian order from the position given it by G. Gracchus was part of the same policy of a supreme Senate.

The soldiers and the freedmen of Sulla held his constitution together while he lived, but with his death war at home and abroad brought a new military leader to the front. The Sullan constitution fell because the Senatorial order were too weak to defend it. The young Pompey who now leapt into prominence had been a protégé of Sulla. Sent to Spain the year after Sulla's death, entrusted with high command without having held any previous office, he was destined, by force of circumstances, to tear to pieces every principle that Sulla had established. Elected direct by the people, as Marius had been, but without holding any magistracy, he ended the war against the remnant of the Marian party in Spain, and returned to lead the popular party against the Senate. After a short interval he received direct from the people extraordinary commands in the East, against the Pirates and then against Mithradates of Pontus. His whole career defied the Sullan rules. But for a time it seemed as though through him the discordant elements in Roman politics might be reconciled. Brought up under the patronage of Sulla, he had wider interests and ties than his master and the legislation which as consul with Crassus he carried in 70 represented a compromise between the old Senatorial traditions and the interests of the capitalists, while it reinstated the prestige of the Tribunate as the organ of popular government. This compromise ultimately failed, from the inherent selfishness of the Senatorial and Equestrian orders and from the inarticulate impotence of the People at large.

The year 70 then must be noted as a critical year for it marks the overthrow of the Sullan reaction, but it brought no new or constructive element to Roman politics, though it may be said to embody the triumph of compromise. That spirit of compromise we find expressed in the speeches and letters of Marcus Tullius Cicero, the great orator and man of letters, whose speeches, letters, and essays provide our fullest evidence for this age. A 'new man',[1] from one of the country families which had from time to time refreshed the Senate with new blood, he expressed the ideas of an educated class which with a respect for the best traditions of Senatorial government combined sympathy for the Italian country towns and for the world-wide interests of Roman finance and commerce. It was in their interest and with their support that as consul in 63 he helped to crush the revolutionary movement of Catiline, which aimed at upsetting credit and society. The tragedy of Cicero's life lay in the fact that Pompey and the Senate by their mutual jealousies refused the combination which might have prolonged Senatorial government and so threw Cicero into the position of hopeless loyalty to a leader and a Senatorial order who had thrown away their opportunity. In 70, the time we are now considering, Cicero was in full accord with Pompey's policy of reversing the reactionary policy of Sulla and supported it with a whole heart. His ideal was a Republic governed by an enlightened Senate, which should give free scope to the Equestrian order. It was his fate that Pompey, whom he respected and followed, neglected him, while Caesar, whom he feared as an enemy of the Republic, treated him with kindness and consideration. But after Caesar's death Caesar's heir, Octavius, was not strong enough to save him from the hatred of Antony, and Cicero fell a victim to his loyalty to the outworn Republic. For Pompey the legislation of 70 was only an incident between his success in Spain and his later triumphs in the East. He had no taste for civil glory and no political gifts.

[1] *novus homo*, i. e. a man whose ancestors had not held high office.

What was the condition of Rome and the Empire when Pompey returned from Asia nine years later, in 61 B.C.?

Italy, as we have seen, had gone through the horrors of prolonged civil war. A slave-rising, too (73–71), like earlier risings in Sicily (135–132, and 103–99), had thrown a lurid light on the social and economic dangers of slavery. In the East, Pompey himself, following on the military successes of Lucullus, a great man unjustly used, had incorporated new provinces in the Empire—Pontus and Syria—besides re-organizing Bithynia. But Rome's hold on Asia Minor had not been completed without a great struggle. In Mithradates, King of Pontus, the Romans found a formidable antagonist, who threatened to sweep them from Western Asia. His massacre of 80,000 Romans [1] in 88 had been the beginning of a long and stubborn struggle extending with intervals over twenty years (first war 88–84, second 74–65), which finally settled the fate of Asia Minor. Western and not Eastern ideas were henceforth to prevail in Western Asia. The Parthian power, which during the Civil wars threatened Roman government in Asia and later became Rome's most formidable enemy, could not entirely destroy the effect of the campaigns of Lucullus and Pompey. It was on their foundation that Augustus when he came to power constructed an Eastern frontier, which, when consolidated by the Flavian Emperors, secured the quiet development of the Hellenic East for many centuries. Pompey, by the new provinces he had added to the Empire, had indicated the main lines of the future frontier system of the East. In the African continent the territory of Carthage had become a province and Numidia had been reduced to a client State. Spain, which for 150 years had cost Rome heavy losses in men and money, was finally reduced in the Numantine War (133) and

[1] This probably includes many Italians who were not full Roman citizens.

in the next century became the most intensely Roman of the Roman provinces. In Gaul a province had been founded in what we now call Provence in 121, to command the highway to Spain, and there a new departure had been taken. The colony of Narbo Martius, the modern Narbonne, founded in 118, was the first transmarine colony founded with full Roman rights, the first of a series of colonies which in the next two centuries were used to Romanize Southern Gaul and Spain and the districts of the Rhine and Danube. But at present and till the end of the Republic the northern frontier was undefined, and Rome had all the anxieties that attend the existence of an unguarded border. The Gallic peril was a commonplace in conversation. Gaul within the Alps, the Cisalpine, was being rapidly Romanized by the bestowal of Latin rights or citizenship, but the districts of the Alps themselves were still half-independent under their chieftains and the country behind (now Switzerland and the Tyrol) was unconquered. The Lombard plain was open to attack. East of the Adriatic the Illyrian country, subject to Rome since the Macedonian conquest, was becoming the province of Illyricum, soon to be held by Julius Caesar along with Gaul, the first of a series of Danubian provinces. Thus the bounds of Empire were coming full circle, but the ring of defence was loosely knit. It is a testimony to the Roman constitution that, through years of civil war and revolution at home, the government of the Empire was going on and provincial governors were succeeding one another, all the world over. Beyond the provinces which were under the direct government of Rome, the policy of a fringe of Client States was still maintained, and as the princes died out, their kingdoms came under the immediate government of Rome. Thus Cyrene, bequeathed to Rome in 96, Bithynia, in 74, became provinces in 74.

The return of Pompey from the East in 61 marks a crisis in

the fortunes of Rome; and we may survey from this point the last act in the drama of the rise and fall of the Republic. Lucan the poet, who died in a so-called Republican conspiracy in the reign of Nero—really a conspiracy to set up a good emperor instead of a bad one—took Pompey as the hero of his *Pharsalia*, and as the embodiment of constitutional rule. The contradiction of Pompey's position was that he posed as the representative of constitutionalism while he claimed powers and privileges which led straight to monarchy. His career was a living contradiction. His coalition with Caesar and Crassus in 60, the 'first Triumvirate', involved an arbitrary partition of the Empire between military commanders which was incompatible with free government. To Caesar this was clear, but Pompey never thought things out, and his equivocal position was his ruin. Caesar used Pompey as a means to acquire a great command for himself, the command of the Gauls and Illyricum. The result was of vast moment in the history of Rome and of Europe. In the strenuous years he spent in the Gallic command Caesar not only achieved the conquest of Gaul and saved Italy from the menace of the northern barbarians, but also created an army, which enabled him to defeat Pompey when the break inevitably came and which formed the foundation of the permanent army of the Empire.[1] How great was the task achieved by Caesar in these years, 59–50, can only be realized by those who have studied the map of France, and the distribution of the tribes which Caesar found in possession. Courage and rapidity of action, organizing capacity, firm control of capable and devoted lieutenants, pitiless severity—these were the qualities which commanded success. There was a moment when the whole fabric of his work threatened to collapse, in the great revolt of 52, the year when at home Pompey began to turn against him, but by the

[1] See *Caesar's Conquest of Gaul* by T. Rice Holmes.

end of 50 when he crossed the Rubicon the work of conquest was complete. Crassus, the third partner, played for himself alone, and found a miserable end, when his severed head was filled with Parthian gold after his defeat by the Parthians at Carrhae. He does not count.

The civil war, which began with Caesar's crossing of the Rubicon in January 49, was in one aspect a contest for supremacy between the rival leaders; in another it was the conflict between Senatorial government and the idea of monarchy which Caesar embodied. The battle was fought between a man who saw his way to consolidate the shaking fabric of the Empire and direct it by wise laws and the government of a strong hand; and the man whose ambitions were beyond his powers, and who was fighting for an outworn constitution, which his own career had done much to undermine. The Senate could not be saved, and the disorders of Pompey's court and camp were a sure prophecy of the last scene on the sands of Egypt, where Pompey found humble burial from a common soldier.[1]

It is significant that the breach between Caesar and Pompey began with a law of Pompey's, the *lex Pompeia de iure magistratuum* of 52, designed to rearrange the system of provincial command, and that the actual outbreak in December 50 was concerned with Caesar's military command in Gaul. Was Caesar or was he not to resign his army and so lay himself open to attack before the year 48, when he hoped, if all was well, to be in a secure position as Consul? Pompey in choosing war, thought he had Italy and the eastern provinces and Client States behind him. Caesar had the advantage of a few highly trained and devoted legions: his rapidity and decision did the rest. Spain and the Balkan peninsula before Pompey's

[1] Pompey, though no statesman, was a great captain. What devotion he could inspire may be seen in the concluding scene in Plutarch's life, which should be read in North's translation.

death—Egypt, Africa, and Asia afterwards, fell into his hands. The Pompeians failed to use their sea-power and none of their leaders had Caesar's genius. In the intervals of these great campaigns, not many months in all, Caesar passed a series of laws which paved the way for ordered government. Besides amnesty to his enemies, there was the settlement of Italy, restoration of credit, reform of the Calendar, rigid repression of revolutionary finance. But he did all this with an authority that defied all rules: combining consulship and dictatorship, appointing to provincial commands, disregarding all conventions, and finally through his friends, asking for open monarchy. His murder was the reply of the Senatorial order. The answer was no answer, for the Republicans who murdered him could not construct a new order nor control the warring passions of Caesar's heirs. The three men who claimed to succeed him, Antony, Octavius, and Lepidus, the Triumvirs of 43, crushed the Republican opposition at Philippi and proceeded to divide the Roman world between them. Lepidus, the third partner, like Crassus in the earlier coalition was no match for the other two and the war became in the end a duel between Antony and Octavius. But before the final conflict, Sextus Pompeius, heir of the great Pompey, had to be disposed of. A master on the sea he was no match for the diplomacy of Antony and Octavius and was finally beaten on his own element by Octavius's trusty lieutenant Agrippa. Republican sea-power now, as in the earlier conflict, failed against the persistency of a Caesar. The treaty of Brundisium (40), which had been cemented by Antony's marriage with Octavia, divided the Roman world between Antony and Octavius, an anticipation of the later division between the Eastern and Western Empires. Antony was the greater soldier, but it became clear that in a struggle of policy against passion, policy would win. Cleopatra captured Antony as she had captured Julius Caesar, though less fatally, before him, and the Roman world recognized in the final clash of arms the conflict not between two Roman generals with equal claims to empire, but a fateful encounter of the forces and ideals of East and West. Virgil in picturing the scene of Actium in *Aeneid VIII* is true to history in the contrast that he draws. On the one side is Augustus (for the poet anticipates the title by four years) leading into battle Italy with the Senate and People of Rome, and their household gods—on the other side is Antony, the leader of a motley host marshalled in barbaric splendour, with an Egyptian bride, and a monstrous train of Oriental deities. The triumph of Augustus Virgil rightly felt to be a triumph of law and disciplined life over the unbridled passions and the unholy worships of the Eastern world. Actium reunited the Empire, which for nine years had been parted between two masters. That momentous battle saved the unity of Rome for five hundred years, and secured the interval for the development of Roman law and government under Augustus and his successors. Had Antony conquered, the ideas and government of the Graeco-Roman world might have been submerged in a flood of Orientalism before they had sown their seed in the nations of modern Europe.

4

From the Accession of Augustus to the Death of Marcus Aurelius

We have seen how the decline of moral in the Senate, and its incapacity to deal efficiently with urgent problems at home and abroad, led to a century of civil strife, in which the whole fabric of the constitution was for a time broken down. The brief monarchy of Caesar had shown what might be done by a single ruler with clear ideas and a strong will. It had also shown that Roman opinion would not tolerate an open monarchy; that the name 'king' was impossible, and that constitutional decencies must be observed. The Principate of Augustus, in which the ruler of the Empire professed to be only the leading citizen in a free state, was an attempt to meet these conditions by a compromise. In the first instance at least it was temporary. The position of 'Princeps' or 'first man in the State' was not a definite office and was not hereditary. Its vagueness was its merit. The various powers on which it rested had precedents in the Republic, but the union of them in one hand was unique and unprecedented. It has been described as a Dyarchy, in the sense of a rule divided between Prince and Senate. In regard to the government of the provinces, the administration of justice, the coinage, Prince and Senate had parallel duties or powers; but the supreme military command, which was superior to the command held by the generals of armies or by provincial governors, combined as it was with the Tribunician power which gave security of person and control of legislation, made the position of Augustus in fact unique and unassailable. Before we attempt to show how these powers developed and what organs the Principate evolved to fulfil its functions, it is necessary to look for a moment at the world which the Princeps was called upon to rule.

Italy had suffered from the campaign between Caesar and Pompey, and still more from the conflicts that followed Caesar's death. Something had been done by the Triumvirs to re-colonize the peninsula, but a large measure of reconstruction remained for Augustus to carry out. In that work he re-founded many old towns of Italy and settled many colonies of citizens abroad. Julius Caesar in his short reign is generally believed to have laid down a type of charter for municipal towns,[1] and

[1] See E. G. Hardy on 'Lex Iulia Municipalis' in *Journal of Roman Studies*, vol. iv, and in *Journal of Philology*, xxxv.

his heir did all he could to promote their active life. He improved communications by restoring roads and bridges, he divided the peninsula into districts (*Regiones*) and by every means encouraged a return to the soil, while the coasts were for the first time efficiently protected from piracy by permanent fleets on the two seas. The removal of the legions to distant frontiers banished the menace of war for a war-weary generation: the institution of the Praetorian guards and the City Cohorts and the Vigiles (a kind of city police and firemen) gave a security to the capital which was in contrast with the discreditable riots and disorders of Rome in the late Republic. The effect of these measures, and in particular the blessed influence of his greatest gift, the gift of peace, was to give Italy something like a century of prosperous life. Senatorial nobles now took to high farming, and real advance was made in agriculture. Capital was invested also in the manufacture of pottery and other wares for export, and for a time the face of Italy was changed. But this air of prosperity was partly fictitious, for now, as in the Republic, much of the apparent wealth of the country consisted of the spoils of the exhausted world, drained of its treasures by one military leader after another. It was unproductive wealth. The free population of Italy was declining, but down to Vespasian there was a partial but genuine revival. This finds its reflexion in the elder Pliny's account of Italian farming and in the statistics of recruiting for the legions, which till Vespasian's time drew men for the Western armies from Italy and particularly from the regions re-colonized by Augustus. But signs of decline began to appear at the end of the first century A.D. in the loans which it is found necessary to make to the farmers and in the charities instituted for the maintenance of the children of needy citizens.[1] Large tracts of country fell out of cultivation

[1] See Mommsen on the *Alimenta* in Bd. II of *Historische Schriften.*

and this led to the spread of malaria, which clung to them till quite recent years: provinces like Gaul competed with Italian manufactures and Italy became more dependent than ever on the subject peoples. Ever since the wars with Macedon, the Italians had enjoyed freedom from direct taxation and this they retained down to Diocletian (284–305), when Italy became one among many provinces. That was the end of free Italy. Even a century earlier the establishment of a Roman legion at Alba, the old capital of the Latins, by Septimius Severus (193–211), was a sign that Italy, like the rest of the Empire, was under direct military rule.

If we look further afield, in the provinces, as in Italy itself, a great constructive work had to be accomplished: in the East the provinces, drained of their treasures by successive armies, had to be nursed into economic stability; in the West and North the newly conquered countries had to be settled; and in both the older and the newer provinces frontiers and a military system had to be organized.

It was part of the great work of Augustus to construct out of the vast armies left in being after Actium a permanent force to defend the frontiers. The old tradition of the Roman army had been to have Romans and their Allies fighting side by side. In the Legions and the auxiliary troops (*Auxilia*) of the Empire this principle was retained. The backbone of both armies was, as it had always been, the centurions, the company officers, drawn from the best Italian material. Among the higher officers the legionary commanders (*Legionum legati*), a creation of Caesar, remained as before, Senatorial: it was a sign that the military monarchy had come into being when the Senate ceased, in Gallienus's reign (259–68), to hold the highest commands. The lower commands, of Tribune and Prefect, were held alike by Equestrian officers qualifying for civil posts and by Senators at the opening of their career. The Legions were recruited partly from Italy (down to Vespasian) but largely and increasingly from the Provinces, and from the Provinces came also the Auxilia, at first under the command of their national officers, but, when experience proved this to be dangerous, under Romans or Italians.

These armies were disposed on the frontiers of the Empire. We must see what these frontiers were, and this means that we have to look beyond Augustus and see how later Emperors completed his work. Let us begin with Asia. To the old provinces in the East, as organized by Pompey, Augustus had added Galatia, and to this were added by Tiberius and organized by the Flavians, Cappadocia and Commagene. This, as will be seen by a glance at the map, brought the frontier up to the Euphrates and prepared the way for a reconstruction of the Eastern defence. From Vespasian onwards the Eastern frontier rested on a double base—Galatia with Cappadocia in the north and the old province of Syria in the south. In the African continent Egypt, which had for fifty years before Actium been a Client-state, became the Emperor's private property, which for safety's sake was kept under the Emperor's personal control. The Emperor named his Viceroy, an Equestrian Prefect, and for administrative purposes retained under him the machinery of the old rule of the Ptolemies. The old division, the Nome, under a Strategus was the unit of administration, and the land tax on the old lines the main source of revenue. The garrison of Egypt was anomalous—one or two legions under an Equestrian instead of a Senatorial commander, so afraid were the Emperors, after Antony's great adventure, of the possible rivalry of a Senatorial ruler. Farther west was Cyrene, next to it the old province of Africa, and two minor provinces of Mauretania organized by Claudius and governed by Procurators: across the strait were the three provinces of Spain, becoming yearly more Roman, and to the north of Spain

Pompeii—Strada dell' Abbondanza.

Pompeii—Strada di Mercurio.

the great new province of the three Northern Gauls, with their capital at Lugdunum (Lyon), while the old province Narbonensis remained under the Senate. Beyond this again were two strips of conquered territory on the Rhine, mere spheres of occupation—Upper and Lower Germany. Eastward of them lay the minor provinces of Rhaetia and Noricum, the hinterland of the Alps, and along the Danube the three provinces of Dalmatia, Pannonia, and Moesia. This region was still further consolidated in Claudius's reign by the annexation of Thrace, which made the whole region south of the Danube a solid block of Roman rule. In the region between the Rhine and Danube, where the great bend northwards of the Rhine makes a re-entrant angle, the territory was occupied by Roman settlers in the first century of the Empire, and the beginnings were made of a *Limes imperii*, a frontier-line connecting the two rivers Rhine and Danube, the eastern part of which survives as the 'Devil's Wall' (Teufelsmauer). Begun by the Flavians it was completed by Hadrian. Only one other extension need be mentioned—one which concerns ourselves: Julius Caesar had made a reconnaissance in Britain and established relations with Client-princes there. Claudius invaded and annexed the island, which remained a part of the Empire for four hundred years. Though the institutions and even the common features of civilized life were swept away by the flood of invading Germans in the fifth century, Professor Haverfield has shown how thoroughly Britain was for the time Romanized.[1] Our Roman roads and the remains of villas, pottery, arms, and utensils, such as may be seen in London at the British Museum or at the Guild Hall, or at Reading, York, or Colchester Museum—still more the Roman Wall in Northumberland, tell their own tale. The

[1] F. J. Haverfield, *The Romanization of Roman Britain*, Clarendon Press.

farthest advance north was made by Agricola in 85,[1] and for some time his advanced position in Scotland was maintained by fortified camps, but later the Roman line of defence was withdrawn first to the line of Forth and Clyde (the wall of Antoninus) and then to the line of Tyne and Solway in its final form (perhaps the work of Severus).

Two advances were made beyond these limits in the period which comes within our view, both in the reign of Trajan—the annexation of Dacia north of the Eastern Danube, and that of Armenia, Mesopotamia, and Arabia to the east of the Euphrates. These eastern conquests were given up by Hadrian as unprofitable, but Dacia was retained for a hundred and fifty years, only to be given up by Aurelian (270–5). The frontier then in this period was a shifting line, and the legions had to be moved from time to time, to suit the new conditions. But, with the exception of the withdrawal from Trajan's advance in the East, the history is in general one of gradual consolidation. The idea once entertained under Augustus of a conquest of Germany was never seriously resumed after the great Pannonian war and the defeat of Varus in A.D. 9, and the main lines laid down by Augustus were adhered to. It was based on the policy of Julius Caesar, who had the genius to conceive a unified control, but had not had time to carry it into effect. A frontier system became possible only with the standing army which Augustus created.

The Rhine and Danube for many years claimed the largest armies, some twelve to sixteen legions: the East was defended by the four legions of Syria, to which were added in Flavian times legions in Judaea and in the united provinces of Galatia and Cappadocia. By that time the garrison of Spain, a highly Romanized province, was reduced to one legion, Africa and

[1] See G. Macdonald in *Journal of Roman Studies*, vol. ix, 'The Agricolan Occupation of North Britain.'

Egypt claimed two or three, and Britain three. These were the forces, varying in different provinces from time to time, that, with about an equal number of Auxiliary troops, defended with the help of rivers, ocean, and desert the extended empire of Rome. There was no field army, and when a fighting force was needed for an emergency, one province had to borrow from another.

Such was the world—from the Atlantic to the Euphrates, and from the Rhine to the Sahara, which Rome had now to govern.

The fall of the Republic, as we have seen, was due to a combination of causes, partly mechanical or structural and partly moral. The machinery of Senatorial government was too rudimentary, the system of government by annual magistracy was unequal to its task: the moral of the Senatorial order had decayed: the new class of capitalists was influential but corrupt and was subject to no control. Finally, the degradation of free labour in Italy and the attractive glamour of the capital had produced a dangerous class in Rome, which through the weakness of Roman criminal law might at any moment make government impossible. The problem of the Principate was to restore and enforce order, to give free play to the new forces and to the best elements in enfranchised Italy and in those provinces which could readily be Romanized, and to create a new machinery of government. But this must be done without shocking Roman sentiment, and in a way which should secure a sense of continuity with the past.

The form which Augustus gave to the Principate did secure this end. The Emperor was the Princeps, the leading man in the State, but the Senate still dealt with a great deal of current business, and no Emperor was fully accepted until chosen by the Senate. The people, it is true, disappear into the background, but we must remember that the Comitia, the Assemblies, which now ceased to meet, had for many years only met to be mischievous if they blocked, and superfluous if they supported, the legislation of the master of the armies. By nomination and commendation the Princeps now controlled the personnel of the Senate, and his choice governed their social existence. Caesar had enlarged the Senate to one thousand: it was now reduced to its old size. Its members had to reside in Rome, and could only go abroad with leave. The magistracies were reorganized and the Senatorial career was defined. There was no lack of public duties.[1] Minor magistracies and a period of qualifying military service as Tribune of a Legion were followed by the serious duties of Praetor and Consul, with the command of a legion or of a Province as the crown of a career. Now as before, the Senator was deemed capable alike of military and civil duty, and passed from one to the other.

Did these officials, it may be asked, belong to the Senatorial nobility of the Republic? Many of the old families had died out, others were too poor to serve; but new families were coming forward from the classes below, and as time went on the Romanized provinces, especially Spain and Gaul, supplied their quota to the new nobility. But the vast business of an Empire could not be dealt with by this class alone. There were two ways in which an advance was made and the personnel of government enlarged. First, the growing needs of the capital and of Italy made it necessary to create new offices of high dignity to control the city of Rome, to take charge of the great lines of communication in Italy, and to look after the water-supply of the capital. These were great Senatorial offices, one of which, the Prefecture of the City, came, in time, to have high judicial duties.

Secondly, the Equestrian Order, the social class below the

[1] For Senatorial careers see Dessau, *Inscriptiones Latinae*, vol. i, cap. 4.

Senatorial, was by degrees converted into a civil service. By a stroke of genius Augustus turned this moneyed class, which had been irresponsible and selfish, to useful and efficient work, by using them, under his personal control, as his agents or proctors—Procuratores and Praefecti—for the conduct of that class of affairs in Rome and the provinces which required some permanence and business capacity and for which the high rank of Senator was either not requisite or not desirable. Thus a very valuable human asset of the Roman world, the trained business class, was saved for the Empire; and a wasting sore of the late Republic was removed. We have only to look at the inscriptions recording the career of some of these great Equestrian officials [1] to see what important offices they filled and with what a wide range of influence. Foremost among these offices was the command of the Guards in Rome. The Prefect of the Praetorians (*Praefectus Praetorii*), the Emperor's Guards, held office alone or with a colleague. This officer naturally exercised a great power in Rome, particularly when the camp of the Guards was established close to the city walls. As the Guards were the only military force near the capital [2] they frequently determined the succession to the throne. But apart from this their central position gave the Prefects of the Guard great power and prestige, and in later days they became judges of appeal for all cases beyond a circle of a hundred miles from Rome. For the narrower sphere of one hundred miles the Senatorial Prefects of the City were responsible. Side by side with the Praetorian Prefects was the Prefect of the corn-supply, the high official whom Augustus had found it necessary to appoint to provide for the feeding of the capital, a vital necessity if the city and the central

[1] See Dessau, op. cit., vol. i, cap. 5.

[2] Except the City Cohorts (*Urbanae Cohortes*), who were under the Prefect of the City, a high Senatorial officer.

government were not to fall a prey to the attack of a hungry rabble in Rome. Abroad the Procurators dealt with the whole range of financial duties except so far as Quaestors survived in the provinces immediately under the Senate. Procurators also held the minor offices subordinate to the high Senatorial commissionerships and curatorships; and finally Procurators (e.g. Felix and Festus) conducted the government of those minor provinces, which the Emperor desired to keep under his immediate control but without entrusting them to Senatorial governors: such as Judaea, Mauretania, Rhaetia, and, most important of all, Egypt.

There were two considerations that made the services of this equestrian class especially valuable. One was that as the Emperor's immediate agents they were completely under his control and were not subject to the rule of annual succession. And secondly, as non-Senators they were excluded from any possible rivalry for the throne.

Just as the Senators had to qualify for civil service by serving first as subordinate officers with the Legions so the Knights had to serve as Tribunes in a Legion or as Prefects in the Auxilia, but they could not rise higher in the army (save in Egypt alone) without passing into the class of Senators.

Beneath these two governing classes of Senators and Knights were the rank and file of the citizens, among whom some of the most capable were the Greek freedmen, whom we meet as conspicuous figures in the early Empire. These were mainly Greeks who had made themselves useful to their masters from their business capacity and cleverness in finance. Already under the Republic, as we see from Cicero's letters, such men had played an active part as private secretaries and confidential agents of provincial governors and high senatorial nobles. Augustus and Tiberius in the main relied on the services of men of Senatorial and Equestrian rank. Maecenas, a knight, had played a great part in the rise of Augustus to power. Seianus, a knight who was Prefect of the Guard, had a disastrous influence over Tiberius. After Tiberius's long absence from Rome, and the short disordered reign of Gaius (Caligula), the cautious Claudius found that the whole fabric of the Empire was in danger of dissolution, for want of firm centralized control, and it was to create this that he gave to the confidential freedmen who governed his household a new position.[1] Men like Pallas and Narcissus held posts which, though unofficial, were highly influential, and they were rewarded by the bestowal of senatorial decorations, though not of senatorial status. At this period these household posts and many of the procuratorships in the Empire were held by freedmen, but this system of freedmen officials proved unsatisfactory, and by the time of Hadrian all such offices were reserved for men of the Equestrian order, whose dignity and status corresponded to their actual services.

While thus provision was made for the personnel of official life, and while central control removed many of the abuses and revived in great measure the efficiency of government, it could not wholly restore the earlier vitality and freedom of the governing class. Two things imposed serious shackles on public life. There was a sense of discomfort in working with a prince whose word, though he professed to be only the first citizen, was felt to be final; whose power unquestioned. This feeling prevented free speech in the Senate and produced an atmosphere of unreality and hypocrisy in which it was difficult to breathe. The machine could only be kept going by occasional suppression of those who still ventured to utter Republican

[1] See Hirschfeld, *Die kaiserlichen Verwaltungsbeamten* (2nd ed. 1905), pp. 471 ff.

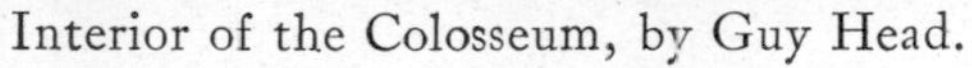

Interior of the Colosseum, by Guy Head.

sentiments or to air their Stoic principles. The astute Augustus had possessed the tact to play his part in the tragi-comedy of the Royal Republic, but the part was a hard part to play and few Emperors played it well. 'The one fear of the Senate', says Tacitus of Tiberius's reign, was 'that they might appear to understand':[1] they did not dare to avow the subjection that they really felt, nor could they be frankly Republican. More serious, perhaps, was the fact that as there was no recognized succession, for outwardly at least there was no definite monarchy, the death of the prince meant certainly danger and possibly revolution. The year of the four Emperors, 69, is the glaring example of the dangers of unavowed monarchy. The Principate did indeed escape some of the evils of a purely hereditary system. It enjoyed from time to time, thanks to adoption, a period of wise and settled government like that of the Antonines. But it was at a heavy cost of uncertainty, and of all the horrors of battle, murder, and sudden death, which uncertainty entailed.

Apart from this inherent weakness there was much that promised well. Law and justice first. The strength of the Roman State, as we saw, rested largely on its law and its judicial system. But 'laws are silent in the clash of arms'[2] and there was much need for reconstruction. We cannot go into detail. It is enough to say that the old standing courts of criminal law, as organized by Sulla, survived, but under a supervision which prevented abuse. By their side were instituted two new high criminal courts—the Senate sitting as a court and the Princeps who sat and decided cases with the help of his Council, selected from the two higher orders. These two courts dealt with all criminal cases which concerned persons of importance,

[1] Tac. *Ann.* i. 11.

[2] 'Silent enim leges inter arma', Cic. *pro Milone*, iv. 10.

and among others all which concerned the doings of provincial governors. Governors still committed crimes, but if they did, they were brought to book. At the same time the civil law, with the widely extended Empire and the increasing business which administration and commerce brought to Rome, continued its development through the Praetorian Edict and the Responsa Prudentium—the authorized opinions given by the great lawyers—and so prepared the way for the great imperial codes of the later Empire. This is a silent growth, which historians too often forget, and it is one of the great works and perhaps the greatest glory of the Empire.

The Empire with its various opportunities of service did call out men's powers. The historians indeed are apt to give us only the morbid side of imperial life—the discontents and discomforts, the vices and the vanities of the capital, the pettiness and the luxury and the oppressive sense of impotence among the governing class. But even through the historians' pages come glimpses of a nobler quality. If the air of Rome was stifling and exhausted, there were great and exhilarating tasks in the defence of frontiers, in the reorganization or Romanization of new provinces, in the just and wise administration of distant and difficult populations. What such a life might mean and how it might appeal not only to men of old senatorial nobility, but to men of newer family who were constantly coming in to reinforce the decaying stocks, may be seen from the lives of men like Corbulo and Virginius Rufus, Agricola and Vespasian. But Corbulo's death showed that to live as a great Senator meant always to live dangerously, and Tacitus's words on the death of Poppaeus Sabinus in 35, a trusted governor of three provinces, are a melancholy reminder that absolute monarchy tends to promote mediocrity: 'for twenty-four years he had been retained in command of important provinces: not for any conspicuous ability that he possessed, but because he was competent and not more than competent.'[1] But competence and justice were not virtues to despise, and for two centuries they did wonders for the Empire. What they did is written in the records of inscriptions in many provinces and of thousands of potsherds and papyri from Egypt. These records recall us to what we have left out of sight for a moment—the local units of government, the town and village life of the Empire. Each province, we must remember, was like Italy, not a uniform surface, but a complex of cities, villages, or tribal units with a variety of rights and privileges. All were subject to tribute unless specially exempted, but while some had Latin or Roman rights with municipal constitutions of the Italian pattern, others were developed on their own peculiar lines: thus Cappadocia and Egypt retained their old divisions into generalships or nomes: Asia and the Greek East in general consisted mainly of cities of the Hellenic pattern with Greek magistrates and council not unlike the Latin magistrates (II viri) and Senate (Decurions) but not leading on, like the Latin type, to Roman citizenship and high imperial service. In Gaul, the old province (Gallia Narbonensis) was intensely permeated by Roman institutions: the North shared Roman culture, but its organization was based on the old canton system, with central towns which grew into important cities but, with rare exceptions, without full Roman or Latin rights: Spain, in every one of its three provinces was steadily and consistently becoming permeated with the Roman type of city life: Africa had important Roman colonies and it also included great imperial estates (*saltus*), and a wide fringe of open country in which hundreds of native tribes had to receive justice and order from the subordinate officials of the Govern-

[1] 'Par negotiis neque supra erat', Tac. *Ann.* vi. 39.

The Palatine from the Colosseum, Rome, by Francis Towne.

ment: the Danubian provinces developed new Roman centres round the great camps and highways. And throughout this vast and varied extent of Empire the Graeco-Roman culture followed the flag. Juvenal's words:

> Gallia causidicos docuit facunda Britannos,
> Glib Gaul has taught the Britains how to plead,

show us how culture passed from Italy to Gaul and thence to Britain. Athens in the east and Massilia (Marseilles) in the west became universities for young nobles from different parts of the Empire.

How the Mediterranean world became unified by Roman government and improved communications is shown by the story of Epictetus and his works. Epictetus, slave and Stoic, came to Rome and taught there. Exiled under Domitian, he lectured at Nicopolis. That we possess his discourses, the lectures that he gave at Nicopolis, is due to the accident that Arrian of Nicomedia in Bithynia, who later rose to high imperial office as governor of Bithynia, attended Epictetus's lectures and published them from his notes. The works of Martial and Seneca bear witness to the culture of Spain. Roman Africa, which French savants have done so much to make known to us, produced the romantic Latin prose of Apuleius, and later on the eloquent utterances of Tertullian and Augustine. But Augustine's 'City of God' carries us beyond the limits we have set for ourselves, into the region of the Christian Empire. In the first two centuries of the Empire we have only to notice that among the influences, philosophic and religious, which were penetrating the Roman world were many faiths which offered new consolation and new hope to a world which had outgrown the early Italian worships and craved for a religion more comprehensive and more cosmopolitan.[1] The Stoic and

[1] Cf. T. R. Glover, *The Conflict of Religions in the Early Empire.*

Epicurean philosophies, the religions of Isis and Mithras and Christ were permeating the society of Rome and the Empire, where Judaism had long before penetrated. The fact of Rome's Empire over the Graeco-Roman world and the communications between Asia and Europe established by the Empire made possible the spread of the Christian faith to Macedonia, Greece, and Italy, and eventually over the whole of Europe. Without that link between East and West afforded by the unity of Roman government, Christianity might have remained a purely Oriental religion. Paul of Tarsus was a Jew, but he was also a Roman citizen, with the rights of a Roman throughout the Empire; but his city was not Roman, but Greek. He is typical of the new relations between Greek culture as modified by Eastern ideas, and the institutions and government of Rome. We cannot trace here the relations between this new religion and the Roman government. They are familiar to all in the narrative of the Acts and in the Apocalypse, and we have glimpses of them in the Roman writers.[1] Acceptable as Christianity was to many men and women in the Empire, especially among the poorer classes, by the appeal it made to wider human sympathies, the dignity it gave to suffering, and among the educated, by its protest against materialism and the worship of power, it was bound to collide sooner or later with Government authority. The Empire allowed a wide latitude in conduct, but was jealous of a society which had no obvious object such as burial or trade-protection; its wide humanity, in which was no respect of persons, and no worship of nationality, made it suspect. The simple test of loyalty to Rome, the outward worship of Rome and the Emperor, was one the Christian could not pass. That is why we find persecution of

[1] Cf. E. G. Hardy, *Christianity and the Roman Government* (in *Studies in Roman History*, 1906).

Christians even under the best Emperors, such as Trajan and Marcus Aurelius, and it did not cease until the gradual permeation of the Empire by the Christian faith made the State recognition of it by Constantine a matter of policy. How these conflicting influences of religion and philosophy were working like a leaven in the Roman world may be seen in Sir Samuel Dill's *Roman Society from Nero to Marcus Aurelius* or in Mr. Glover's book on the conflict of religions, or in a more personal form in Dr. Edwin Abbott's *Silanus the Christian* and Pater's *Marius the Epicurean.*

Throughout the first two centuries of the Empire many regions of Europe enjoyed peaceful growth and development under the Roman rule. The frontiers were consolidated, life flourished in many hundreds of communities of Latin or Hellenic type :[1] trade and culture were spread as wide as the Roman world. But even in this period signs of decline began to appear. Italy fell away in population and productiveness. Large tracts of the land in Italy and the provinces became absorbed in enormous estates (*saltus*) which gradually fell under imperial control, and became the home of a new type of tenant, the *coloni*, fixed to the soil and performing stated duties to the lord, an anticipation of the villeinage of the Middle Ages. Centralized administration became more rigid, local life languished and had to be inspected and reformed and bolstered up by imperial commissioners and public subsidies. The local senates all over the Empire became responsible for the collection of taxes. Municipal service thus became a pure burden, and local production broke down under imperial charges. The blighting influence of a bureaucracy which became more

[1] For Municipal Life, see Dessau, op. cit., vol. ii, 1, cap. xiv ; E. G. Hardy, *Roman Laws and Charters* ; J. S. Reid, *Municipalities of the Roman Empire* ; T. W. Arnold, *Roman Provincial Administration.*

The Segovia Aqueduct.

exacting as agriculture and commerce became less productive, gradually dried up the springs of life. Meantime the enemies without, Germans and Sarmatians in the north, Parthians in the east, in spite of the repeated effort spent on the organization of frontiers, exercised a continual pressure, which meant continuous expenditure on war and on defensive lines.

The reign of Marcus Aurelius, a philosophic lover of peace, was largely taken up with a more or less continuous conflict with the tribes of the North—Quadi, Marcomanni, and the rest. His *Meditations* were written in the exile of border campaigns. In A.D. 166, some three hundred and fifty years after its foundation as a Latin colony to guard the eastern gate of Italy, Aquileia was besieged by invading Germans. Though the Emperor's coins bore the title a few years later of 'Germany subdued', the Emperor's scheme for new provinces beyond the northern frontier had to be abandoned and, instead, a large body of German settlers were planted within the Empire. This was no new thing, but it marked a stage in the process by which the population of the northern provinces was gradually modified by peaceful penetration, until the Empire became the easy prey of the invading barbarians.[1]

We saw that with the destruction of Corinth and Carthage in 146 B.C. the era of Revolution began and with it the presage of the monarchy. There is a memorable symmetry in the fact that A.D. 146, nearly three hundred years later, was the year of the birth of L. Septimius Severus,[2] with whose reign the military monarchy definitely began. After the reign of Marcus Aurelius's worthless son Commodus, and the brief power of

[1] See *Letters of Sidonius Apollinaris* (A.D. 431–89), translated by O. M. Dalton, Clarendon Press.

[2] See *The Life and Reign of Septimius Severus* by M. Platnauer, Clarendon Press.

Pertinax, it was the task of Septimius Severus to reorganize the military forces of the Empire. The reconstruction he accomplished cost a heavy price. From now onwards Italy lost the free and commanding position she had held in the Empire; the Senate became a mere appendage and echo of the Emperor, whose guards no longer represented the flower of Italian manhood, but were drawn from victorious legions of the Danube. The military autocracy was marked by the legion stationed at Albano, the old centre of the Latin League. The wheel had come full circle. Rome had first climbed to power in Latium as the successor of Alba Longa. Since the dissolution of the Latin League in 338 B.C. she had gradually acquired control first over Italy and then over all the Mediterranean lands. For five hundred years Rome had spread her civil government wherever her arms had conquered, and when the Republic was succeeded by the monarchy, one of the signs of the Augustan Peace and of the return of civil rule was the removal of the army to the frontiers. The legion planted on the Alban hills was a sinister sign that Rome had come under military rule and that Italy henceforward was to be little more than one among many provinces. For five hundred years Rome had propagated the principle of self-governing communities within an expanding territory, ruled by Roman magistrates and Roman law, and defended by Roman armies. This vital principle had achieved great results: it had created a united empire in which, amid many diversities of structure Graeco-Roman culture was made widely accessible and Roman law was administered to all. But from the moment when Rome began to hold territories beyond the sea, the taint of selfish exploitation entered the fabric of the State. The rule of the early Principate, as we have seen, redressed many of the grievances of the subject provinces, but even so their tributary position imposed on them a heavy burden. Though the wide extension of Roman and Latin rights opened an avenue to the service of the Empire for provincials from many lands, the provinces as political units had no share in imperial government. The Provincial Councils [1] were little more than religious assemblies: they might represent their grievances to Rome, but they had no effective power. The position of Rome and Italy, dependent on a toiling world beyond the seas, was unnatural and unhealthy, and its economic and moral decline was reflected in the gradual growth of an over-staffed bureaucracy, the substitution of fussiness for vitality, and the final domination by the army over a senatorial order which had lost its governing manhood and was rapidly becoming a mere court nobility. The monarchy of Diocletian with its elaborate hierarchy of officials, its sub-divided provinces and economic regulations, was only the logical fulfilment of a process which was squeezing the life out of the Empire. New life could only come from the more vigorous races of the barbarian world outside. This is not the place to trace the fall of the Empire. With all its defects it had saved Graeco-Roman civilization for some centuries. The new nations which ultimately broke in upon its life inherited in Roman law and institutions influences which have profoundly moulded the fabric and the life of modern Europe.

Looking back we have to ask what are the features of Roman history which dwell in our minds and what constitutes Rome's claim to greatness?

We must put first the vigour and vitality of the race, which was the primary foundation of its emergence from the other peoples of Italy. Next, its genius for command. The command, *imperium*, of the Roman magistrate, was strong and

[1] E. G. Hardy, *Studies in Roman History* (first series).

rooted in a deep sense of order and discipline. Moreover, it showed itself capable of adaptation and adjustment to many services—home and foreign, civil and military, judicial and administrative. It was the directing and controlling force in the State. But the magistrate's power was nothing if not backed up by the counsel and support of its advisers. It was the fundamental principle of Rome that the magistrate must take advice. Out of this advice, *consilium*, and the picked assembly of advisers, was evolved the might and majesty of the 'Assembly of kings' as an enemy called it, the Roman Senate. Further, by its skilful adaptation of the City-state to the conditions of a sovereign people, governing first Italy and then an extended empire, Rome invented municipal life—the reconciliation of local and imperial government. It is true that the reconciliation to our minds was incomplete. Rome never invented a representative system. The towns of the Empire remained without a voice (except through individual members not selected by them) in the conduct of imperial affairs. But even as it was the Roman municipal system was a great creation.

Finally, through its judges and lawyers, working from generation to generation to adapt legal ideas to a perpetually expanding polity, a noble system of law was built up for the use of the world.

And if we turn to the spiritual side of life, and ask what Rome contributed, what are we to say? The creative ideas in science and art, it must be admitted, belong to Greece, though we are beginning to realize that Greece, too, owed something to those who went before. The early Roman religion, like the worship of ancestors in China, added a dignity and sanctity to family life, but the religion and philosophy of the later Republic and Empire was drawn from Greece and the East. Rome's literature, too, looked eastward, but no one can say that Lucretius and Virgil, Catullus and Horace and Juvenal, Tacitus and Seneca, have not distinctive qualities which mark a masterly and independent race. On architecture and engineering the Romans left a lasting impress, and in historic sculpture,[1] in noble portraiture and the rendering of great moments of history in bronze and stone, still more in the inscriptions which record men's lives—they were masters of the grand style.

They showed at times the hardness and unscrupulousness which few expanding nations have entirely escaped; but that must not blind us to their great virtues. To sum up their greatness in a word is not easy, but it is perhaps enough to point to three single works that illustrate their power—the *Aeneid* of Virgil, the marble sculptures of the *Ara Pacis* that record the Peace of Augustus, and their noblest monument of all—the Roman Law. But beyond and above particular monuments is the tradition of a manly national character, nurtured to noble issues by the discipline and pieties of a wholesome family life: strong in natural affections and in a high sense of public service: a national character which found expression in the lives of thousands of dutiful citizens (whose portraits in the museums of Italy appeal to us with so close a kinship), and in institutions which, at their best, brought order, security, and justice to the nations of the earth.

[1] See Mrs. Arthur Strong, *Roman Sculpture*, pp. 40 foll.

Printed in England at the Oxford University Press.

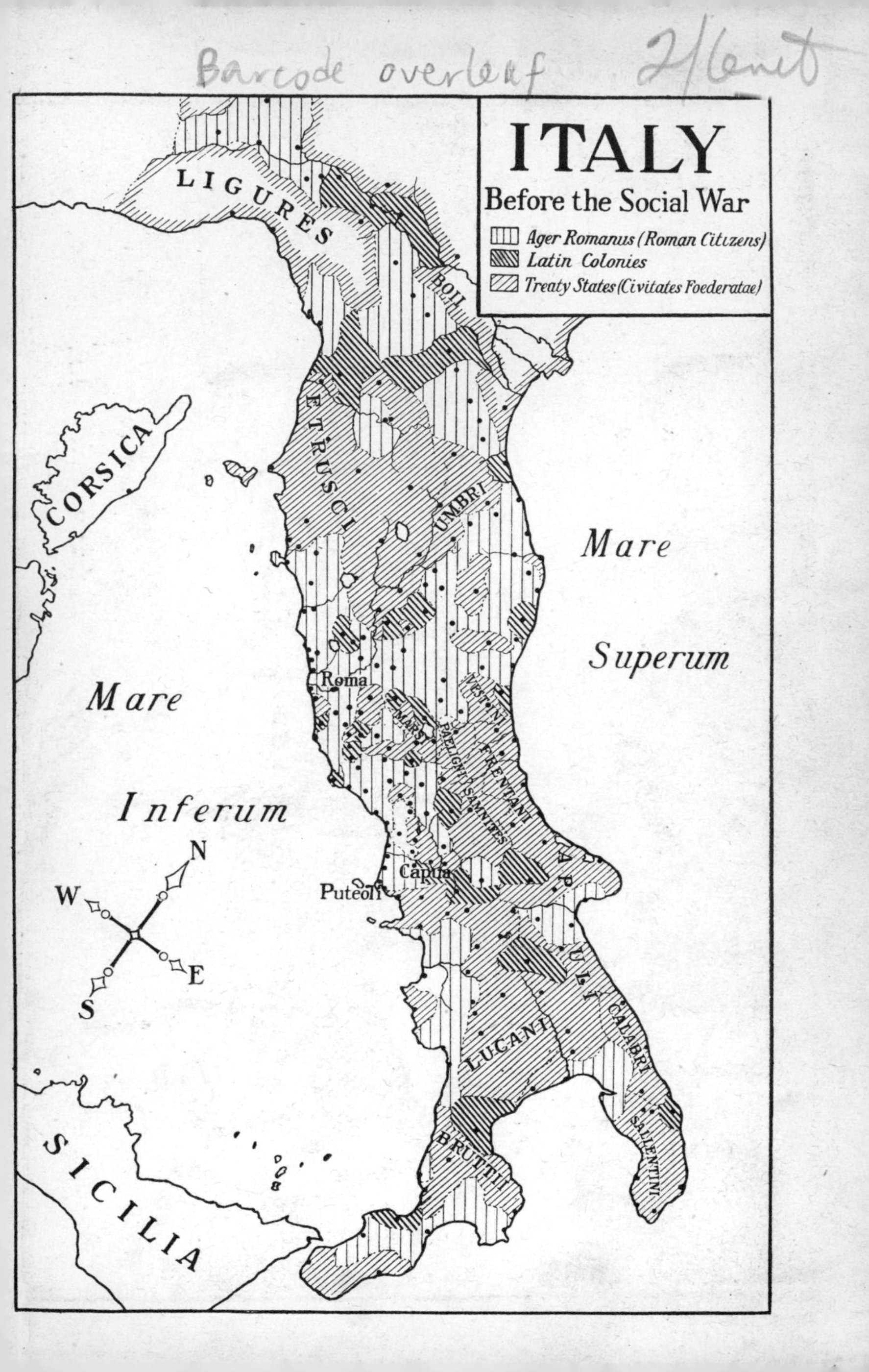
ITALY
Before the Social War
Ager Romanus (Roman Citizens)
Latin Colonies
Treaty States (Civitates Foederatae)
LIGURES
BOII
ETRUSCI
UMBRI
CORSICA
Mare
Superum
Roma
Mare
Inferum
VESTINI
MARSI
PAELIGNI
FRENTANI
SAMNITES
Capua
Puteoli
APULI
LUCANI
CALABRI
SALENTINI
BRUTTII
SICILIA
N
W
E
S